THE COUNTRY LIFE LIBRARY OF ANTIQUES

LONGCASE CLOCKS

THE COUNTRY LIFE LIBRARY OF ANTIQUES

Longcase Clocks

John McDonald

COUNTRY LIFE BOOKS

Frontispiece
Fine clock in slim walnut and marquetry case;
by Joseph Windmills, London, *c.* 1690.

To Renée

Published by Country Life Books
and distributed for them by
The Hamlyn Publishing Group Limited
London . New York . Sydney . Toronto
Astronaut House, Feltham, Middlesex, England

First published 1982
ISBN 0 600 32103 7

Set in 10pt Monophoto Garamond by
Tameside Filmsetting Limited, Ashton-under-Lyne.
Printed in England by Hazell, Watson and
Viney Limited, Aylesbury.

Contents

CHAPTER ONE

The Companionable Grandfather

THIS IS A BOOK about grandfather clocks, more properly known as longcase clocks, those tall, dignified timekeepers admired and loved by so many people. These great clocks, with the patina of the years on their cases and their dials – gilded, silvered or painted in styles of the past – lend an air of antiquity to any room.

In *c.* 1675, when Charles II was king of England, Sir Richard Legh of Lyme Park, Cheshire wrote to his young wife from London concerning the proposed purchase of a clock. He said:

I went to the famous Pendulum maker, Knibb, and have agreed for one finer than my father's and it is to be better finished with carved capitalls gold and gold pedestalls with figures of boys and cherubimes all brass gilt. I took their advice to have it black ebony which suits your Cabinett better.

His wife replied: 'As for the Pandalome case I think Black suits anything.' With a delightful disregard for spelling these two were discussing a longcase clock, sometimes referred to in the late 17th century as a 'Pendulum'. At no time did they mention the words 'grandfather clock' for the name did not then exist and would not for another 200 years when the Victorians adopted the term from Henry C. Work's popularly sentimental song about the grandfather clock which was never to go again after its owner died. These favourite furnishings for so many centuries have always been known as longcase clocks.

A certain amount of controversy has existed among antiquarian horologists as to which nation first produced the longcase clock. Certainly the Dutch had them about the same time as the English, but who was first in the field has never been satisfactorily determined. While there were no longcase clocks in England before 1660, they certainly did appear soon after the Restoration of the Monarchy in that year.

1. Beautifully designed
dial of Knibb clock with
rare skeleton chapter ring
having every minute
individually engraved.

Clock historians who have made a particular study of longcase
clocks used to maintain that they evolved from a need to protect the
mechanism of the wall lantern clock from dust and from careless
passers-by who might knock the weights and so disrupt the
running of the clock. A square wooden hood with a glazed front,
so that the dial could be seen, might have been placed over the wall
clock and this was very likely how the hooded clock came into
being; the addition of a long narrow case enclosing the weights and
ropes would have been another logical step to protect the clock,
the result being a longcase clock. However, because the longcase
clock appeared on the scene about the same time as the hooded
clock, it is almost certain that the design of the former was spon-
taneous.

The popularity of the longcase clock lasted nearly two centuries
from its introduction until Victorian times. By the 1950s longcase
clocks were literally being given away, but today the story is quite
different. Due to the great interest in antiques which has developed
over the last twenty years, the stately longcase clock once again has
pride of place in the home of many a collector. Its slow, measured
ticking and the hourly striking on a bell or gong, is a treasured and
very real link with the past.

Whether or not the longcase clock originally came from Holland,
there is no doubt that the Dutch clockmakers first adapted the

8

pendulum for time control on clocks. A young London clock-maker, John Fromanteel, entered the employment of Salomon Coster, master clockmaker at The Hague, in 1657. There he learned how the pendulum could be integrated with the movement of a clock; a year later Fromanteel was back in London producing pendulum clocks and shortly after the first longcase clocks appeared.

John Fromanteel had a famous brother, Ahasuerus, who was also a clockmaker and who collaborated with Huygens, the Dutch astronomer and mathematician, in designing pendulum clocks.

Clock collecting has been the pastime of many famous people, including Charles II. John Evelyn, the well-known 17th-century diarist, recorded that, adjoining the bedroom where the king lay

2. Walnut veneered longcase clock by Christopher Gould, London – a maker of great repute, who died in 1702.

3. (*Above*) Gould dial with cavetto moulding under hood suggesting that this was one of his last clocks.

9

4. Outstanding walnut marquetry clock with month movement; by John Knibb, Oxford, c. 1680.

dying in 1685, there was a little closet of curiosities containing nearly 100 clocks which Charles had gathered together. From the time of the introduction of domestic clocks into England during the reign of Henry VIII, the continued acquisition of fine horological specimens over the centuries has made the Royal clock collection world famous. A magnificent walnut clock with a year movement by Thomas Tompion, made c. 1695 for William III, is illustrated in this chapter. The well-known late 17th-century maker, Daniel Quare (1649–1724), was commissioned to make a clock for William III and this one-year longcase is now at Hampton Court. Thomas Tompion made another longcase clock for the same monarch which has a three months duration movement and a perpetual calendar. Many other makers received similar royal commissions, like Joseph Antram (d. 1723), who was clockmaker to George I.

George III was keenly interested in clocks and is said to have personally intervened in the controversy surrounding the award made to John Harrison (1693–1776) for his chronometer to be used in calculating longitude at sea.

Another fine maker, third of a generation of reputable producers of fine clocks, was Benjamin Lewis Vulliamy (1780–1854). He was also a royal clockmaker, but his reputation suffered in the present century when it became more widely known that he had virtually vandalised many fine clocks in the Royal Collection. This he had done by substituting his own movements, which he considered to be vastly superior, for the original ones made by outstanding makers of the late 17th and early 18th centuries.

As styles in furnishings and interior decoration are often referred to by the period when a particular king or queen reigned, it can be an advantage to develop a sort of time scale in the mind for easy reference when examining clocks. The rise and decline in the fashion for longcase clocks occupied approximately 200 years of British history; these years divide conveniently into two equal parts—1660 to 1760 and 1760 to 1860—and may be subdivided as follows:

1660–85	Charles II	Restoration or Carolean period
1685–8	James II	
1689–1702	William and Mary	William and Mary period
1702–14	Queen Anne	Queen Anne period
1714–27	George I	Early Georgian period
1727–60	George II	Early and Mid-Georgian periods
1760–1820	George III	Late Georgian period until 1810, thereafter Regency period
1820–30	George IV	Regency period
1830–37	William IV	
1837–60	Victoria	Early Victorian period
1860–1900	Victoria (d. 1901)	Late Victorian period

5. (*Left*) Red japanned clock by Nathaniel Style, London, 1725–73 – good maker and Master of Clockmakers' Company 1751.

6. Dial of Style clock with urn-and-flower spandrels, but later replacement hands.

When a new invention, particularly something of a mechanical nature, makes an appearance, it is usually improved by modification and development almost indefinitely. This may be said to be true of clocks in general, but, as far as fine design and superlative craftsmanship is concerned, the longcase clock reached its peak by the end of the 17th century and from then on, until its virtual disappearance in mid-Victorian times, the period was one of slow but inevitable decline. The proportions and decoration of the case, the design of the dial and its component parts, the chapter ring, the hands, the spandrels, the subsidiary dials – all were models of functional and artistic design to a degree seldom reached after the beginning of the 18th century. This is a generalisation, and there were exceptions, as the work of London clockmakers and of a number of those producing clocks in provincial towns was maintained at a satisfactory standard during the long Georgian period. There can be little doubt that the first forty years of the history of the longcase clock was the time when the finest work was achieved – the reason why clocks of this period are so much sought after by collectors and why they command such high prices.

The period of the Restoration in England was a time when not only the fine and decorative arts – like architecture, painting, silver-smithing, furniture-making and so on – were flourishing, but when there was also an increasing appetite for things of a scientific nature. The Greenwich Observatory was established in 1675 so that astronomy could be studied in greater detail with the prime aim of establishing methods for improving navigation at sea. It was due to advances made in these studies, ably assisted by the accuracy of the clocks designed and made by the clockmakers of the time, that the British were eventually enabled to achieve a foremost position among the nations of Europe as a major colonial and trading power in the following century. Sir Isaac Newton and other philosophers and mathematicians were discovering and formulating laws of nature, such as gravitation. Paving the way for all this activity in the sciences was the founding of the Royal Society, its Royal Charter being granted in 1662. It was soon realised that the exploration of so many scientific avenues required, above all, accurate time measurement. From then on clockmakers vied with each other to produce clocks which would keep extraordinarily accurate time, in some cases achieving an accuracy unequalled until the development of the atomic clock. The ownership of a domestic clock had, until 1700, always been the prerogative of the well-to-do; until the middle of the 18th century clocks were found in comparatively few households. Of thirty-eight inventories of goods and chattels listed at Richmond, Yorkshire between 1660 and 1700 only three included clocks. One inventory of 1689 mentioned a clock, a 'payre virginalls' (an early keyboard musical instrument) and a 'Jack' for roasting meat before a fire. The clock was probably a brass lantern and the three items together were valued at £1 10s. In 1672 an alderman of Richmond named William Wetwange had in his possession '1 clock and the case £2 10s'. This was almost certainly a longcase clock with one hand, a thirty hour movement and a simple oak case. In another will of 1701, for which an inventory had been prepared, there is listed '1 clock out of repair with a case 15s'. Obviously, if you had a clock in those days you were somebody.

7. Green and gold japanned
clock, faded to old bronze
colour, by William
Kipling, London,
1705–37.

The valuation placed on the clocks mentioned above seems
today to be rather small and it might appear strange that more
people did not possess them. On the other hand, the following list
of items made out in 1673 for Henry Broderick consisted of the
entire furnishings for his 'Parler' and were valued at £3 5s. and
clearly illustrates the value of money then. They included:

One Table, one Counter, one silver bowl, one dresser, one chest, four
chairs, five stools, one 'dubler' [?], two candlesticks, one old warming
pan, one Seeinglass [magnifying glass?], six cushions with other things.

8. Domed arch hood and
dial of Kipling clock with
original hour hand, but
doubtful minute hand.

Nearly 100 years later, in 1794, a clockmaker in Bury St Edmunds
was advertising:

Best new Eight Day clocks in square cases, either wainscott or walnutree,
at £5. The same in arched cases at £5 5s. New eight day clocks in
mahogany cases at £6 6s. The same with moon plates, at £6 16s. 6d.
Thirty hour clocks with minutes and day of the month, in wainscot or
walnutree cases, at £3 15s. 6d.

These prices might at first seem absurdly low; but remembering
that a clerk at the Liverpool Herculaneum Pottery received in
salary only 60 guineas per annum in 1808, these late Georgian
longcase clocks were not so cheap after all.

CHAPTER TWO

The Lenticle Door (Charles II)

THE FIRST LONGCASE clocks produced in England shortly after 1660 were notable examples of almost perfect design. The cases were about six feet in height and quite narrow with pedimented hoods showing distinct architectural influence. The dials and hands were models of good taste with no excess decoration that would interfere with telling the time. Early cases were made of pine or fruitwood, which was stained black or ebonised, as the process was termed, and then wax polished.

Soon, however, the demand for more extravagant finishes brought into use the recently introduced process of veneering. Basic furniture constructions of ordinary reliable woods of no significant attraction or character were covered with a thin layer of a more exotic timber notable for its colour, interesting grain and rarity. The practice of veneering brought into being a whole range of more attractive pieces of furniture which were to be still further enhanced by insetting the veneers with small panels of marquetry.

Marquetry work consisted of applying a carefully drawn out pattern, usually birds-and-flowers, to several sheets of different coloured veneers. These were pinned together and the pattern was carefully cut out with a fine-toothed framesaw until it formed a sort of jigsaw puzzle. The craftsman sat astride a type of narrow stool, known as a 'markatree cutter's donkey'. This had a vertical vice at one end which held the veneers being sawn into a marquetry pattern. The various pieces were then re-arranged so that a contrast was formed with the coloured veneers. If four sheets of veneer had been used for the process, then four separate panels of marquetry would result. Thin paper was then pasted over each panel to hold the pieces together and the marquetry sheet was glued onto the front of the clockcase door or any other parts which were to be decorated. The point should be made here that the marquetry is laid onto the surface, not inlaid.

9. Detail of Knibb miniature movement with what may be the earliest example of anchor escapement on a domestic clock.

10. (*Right*) One-hand ebonised longcase, *c.* 1680, with cresting on hood and alarm setting disc in dial centre. Museum of the Worshipful Company of Clockmakers, Guildhall, London.

Earlier examples were designed in smaller panels, outlined with boxwood stringing (narrow square-section strips of wood) and surrounded by areas of walnut veneer. Gradually, as Restoration fashions became more flamboyant, the coloured flower motifs were used to cover the entire front areas of the longcase clock; this is usually referred to as 'all-over' marquetry.

Veneers were also cut to take advantage of any unusual colour or figuring in the grain. This was used, as in cross-banding (cut across the grain), to provide a strip of veneer at right angles to the main panel; it is found around the edges of the veneered sides of the case and sometimes on the trunk door itself. As veneers were cut from a block of wood, the sheets tended to have the same pattern of figuring with only very slight differences in the grain. Four pieces could then be glued into position with the similar grain patterns arranged to form what is known as quartered veneer. The smaller branches of some hardwood trees like walnut and olive have a light and dark sap and heartwood colouring. When cut into thin slices and with the additional marking of the annual rings, the small round or oval veneers can be pieced together to form a pattern known as oyster-shell veneering.

On some ebony-veneered cases, gilded ormolu mounts were used to ornament the polished, black surfaces of the hood and also for the capitals and bases of the miniature architectural columns which were fitted to the hood doors. One of the characteristics of Restoration furniture design, which was indicative of the Baroque style, was the 'barley sugar' or spiral twist. This was used on chair backs, rails and also on the legs of side tables and cabinet stands. Spiral-twist columns are also found on more elaborate late 17th-century clock case hoods.

About 1680, carved crestings, often with the popular device of a winged cherub head, were fitted to the tops of clock case hoods when the triangular pediment shape gave way to a flat top. This custom remained in fashion for only a short time and, because the crestings were simply fitted to the hoods with loose pegs, they were easily detached and lost during house removals. An original cresting on a longcase clock of this period is something of a rarity.

During the early years following the introduction of the longcase clock, the movements were equipped with short bob pendulums combined with a verge escapement. Shortly before 1670 a pendulum measuring 39.1 inches in length appeared, which had a singular characteristic in that its swing or vibration took exactly one second. Because of the importance of this attribute, the new pendulum for longcase clocks was to form the basis of the reputation which they were to enjoy for almost perfect time-keeping and it was named the 'Royal' pendulum. However, it could not be used with a verge escapement, the arc of the vibration being far too great. Soon, a new type of escapement was invented which was to prove the ideal counterpart for the long pendulum since it ensured a swing of only a few inches. Because of its shape, it became known as the 'anchor' escapement.

The association of the Royal pendulum with the anchor escapement and the question of to whom the credit for their invention was to be given, has produced much controversy among antiquarian horologists over the years. It has never been proved really satisfactorily who the actual inventor was. At one time the attribution was given to Dr Robert Hooke, a remarkable Restoration scientist, who came from a very humble background. As a young man he pursued an M.A. degree course as a servitor at the University of Oxford; that is, he performed certain duties in return for his tuition. He had the good fortune to attract the attention of Dr Seth Ward and, under his direction, Hooke soon earned a reputation for his scientific experiments, including several connected with pendulums. Because of this he is still held by many to have been the inventor of the Royal pendulum. In the same year as the Royal Society was formed, 1662, Dr Hooke became its Curator and eventually Secretary in 1677.

The invention of the anchor escapement has also been attributed to a famous London clockmaker, William Clement, who was Master of the Clockmakers' Company between 1694 and 1699. In 1671 he made a turret clock for King's College, Cambridge, which had an anchor escapement and this is thought to have been the first time such an escapement was incorporated in a clock movement. There are sceptics, however, who consider it may have been a later modification. Clement is thought by some to have been the inventor of the Royal pendulum as well. Certainly, he was the first to suspend the long pendulum with a fine strip of flexible spring steel which was known as a 'feather'. At present honours are divided. Hooke has the Royal pendulum and Clement the anchor escapement. The story is a fascinating 'whodunit' from the world of antique clocks.

The advent of the Royal pendulum brought about an increase in the width of clock cases in order to accommodate the larger pendulum bob which now swung well down inside the trunk. To maintain overall good proportion the height of the clock case had to be increased to a little over seven feet.

Now an addition was made to the trunk door in the form of a small circular or oval window called a lenticle which was situated at the height of the pendulum bob. The bob was covered with polished brass so that it could be clearly seen swinging from side to side. Early lenticles were made of plain glass, but in later country-made clocks they often had 'bull's-eye' glass. This was thought to be functional as it magnified the glint of the pendulum bob but, in fact, the 'bull's-eyes' could be obtained more cheaply and although they have a certain attraction it is possible that, where they are found in better type longcase clocks, they are later replacements. The lenticle door on longcase clocks remained in fashion until the end of the first quarter of the following century by which time it seemed that owners of longcase clocks no longer required any reassurance about the reliability of the movements. Apart from appearing occasionally on the doors of country-made, one-hand clocks in simple oak cases later in the 18th century, a

11. Anonymous brass dial, with unusual 'zig-zag' engraving now traceable to Richard Gilkes, Adderbury, Oxfordshire, c. 1740.

lenticle remains a useful pointer in dating a clock between 1675 and 1725.

At the time of the Restoration the normal period of going time for any clock was thirty hours which allowed for daily winding plus a few extra hours if this was delayed. Clocks of a longer duration then began to appear and the eight-day clock, to be wound once a week, became the standard type for domestic use although the thirty-hour type still remained a favourite in the country for a very long time to come.

The first Restoration thirty-hour longcase clocks and many early 18th-century examples had an hour hand only, which indicated the hours and quarters on graduations engraved on the inner edge of the dial chapter ring. These single hour hands may be recognised by a tail which was used to assist in adjusting the hand for the correct time and minimised any chance of breakage. With the advent of the eight-day clock the minute hand was also introduced together with minute markings between the hour numerals. These were engraved on a band near the outer edge of the chapter ring. Minute hands are also found occasionally on a better type of thirty-hour clock of the period. The seconds pendulum now permitted the addition of a seconds hand, literally a second minute hand, with a small seconds dial which was placed immediately above the main dial centre.

A further innovation about this time was the introduction of a self-changing calendar on the clock dial. The date was shown each day through a small hole or calendar aperture, the thirty-one days of the month being engraved on a flat ring which turned on small grooved supporting wheels behind the calendar aperture. The calendar ring had a toothed inside edge which engaged in a trip mechanism every twenty-four hours; this turned the ring and presented the next date numeral at the aperture. The change-over can be set to occur in the small hours of the night so that even an early riser could begin the day with the correct date. The calendar ring has to be moved manually to adjust for those months of the year which have less than thirty-one days.

The shape of the calendar aperture may be taken into account when attributing a clock to a particular period. Square or ringed circular holes, placed below the centre of the dial were usual before the middle of the 18th century, while larger openings in the shape

12. (*Left*) Country-made thirty-hour one-hand clock in simple oak case; by Smallwood, Macclesfield, *c.* 1740.

13. (*Top*) Tompion dial – numerals inside minute band and simple cherub spandrels denote late 17th-century date.

14. (*Above*) Although crown and boys spandrels and hands indicate the 1700 to 1720 period, large minute numerals suggest later date.

of an arc of a circle, and which showed several date numbers at a time, are commonly found after 1760. A small indicator at the top of the arc opening points to the exact day number.

Mention has already been made of the good taste and restraint exercised by the early makers in the design of longcase clocks and this was well demonstrated in the brass dials of the first ebony-veneered examples. These dials were small, about nine or ten inches square with silvered chapter rings attached. The chapter ring, so called because of its monastic associations in bearing originally the divisions of the canonical hours which preceded the partition of the day into twenty-four equal hours, was divided into twelve equal parts with the numbers of the hours engraved in Roman numerals. The word 'dial' was derived from the Latin word 'dies' meaning a day. Small Arabic numbers were also engraved within a band near the outer edge of the ring, which carried minute divisions. These small figures in sets of five, from 5 to 60, within the minute band are characteristic of an early date of manufacture. By 1690 the Arabic numerals were taken out of this position and placed along the outer edge of the chapter ring and from then on they gradually increased in size throughout the following century until they became nearly as large as the Roman hour figures.

The space between the rectangular corners of the dial and the arc of a circle of the chapter ring is known architecturally as a spandrel. These corner areas were at first filled with engraved patterns of flowers and ribbons, but by 1670 separate castings in brass of winged cherub heads, carefully chased and gilded, were attached to provide decoration to the dial. From then on the attached castings became known as spandrels and patterns peculiar to certain period styles provide further evidence of dates of manufacture. The area of the dial within the circle of the chapter ring was finely matted to provide a dull surface against which the dark, blue-coloured and delicately fretted hour and minute hands could be clearly seen. Apart from the winding holes there were no other features on these early dials to detract from the main function of telling the time. The subsequent additions of calendar apertures, ringed winding holes and further engraving on the dial centre were to gradually obscure the beautifully restrained design of the first longcase dials.

The London Clockmakers' Company received its charter in

1631, control of the trade being among its aims. One regulation was that the maker's name should appear on the dial; this was discreetly complied with by engraving the particulars along the lower edge, thus preserving the essential simplicity of the dial itself. The earliest inscriptions were carried out in Latin, as became an object of academic interest, and names like 'Edwardus East Londini' or 'Thomas Tompion Londini' are found together with the occasional addition of the word 'fecit' meaning 'he made it'. A variation of this form of inscribing the maker's name was to surround it with a scroll or cartouche placed slightly below the dial centre; but the introduction of the calendar aperture caused the maker's name to be removed to the lower part of the chapter ring where it appeared on either side of the six o'clock numeral.

The first longcase clocks had a glazed front to the hood, but no door was fitted. When the clock required to be wound or the hands adjusted then the hood had to be moved upwards. It was made to slide in vertical grooves at the back and could be locked in the lowered position by a catch known as a 'spoon' because of its similarity to a spoon handle. This prevented unauthorised persons altering the position of the hands. When the height of longcase clocks was increased after the introduction of the Royal pendulum, c. 1670, it became difficult for the average person to manipulate the upward-sliding hood. To give access to the dial a glazed door was now attached to the front of the hood which was also made to slide forward and lift off when an inspection of the clock movement was required to be carried out.

Until the end of the 17th century all longcase clock hoods were supported on a moulding which was always convex in shape and veneered or decorated with marquetry according to the design of the case. Convex mouldings, like the spiral twist, were a characteristic of Restoration furniture design and are found on items such as the heavy, convex mirror frames of that period. Another aspect of longcase clock design was the absence of a plinth around the base of some cases and the provision of small bun feet instead. These were similar to the larger bun feet on chests of drawers, cabinets and other box-like structures of the period. The chance discovery of a complete example proved that these earlier longcase clocks with bun feet had a pedestal-like tray on which they stood. Unfortunately, being separate items, they have almost all been lost

15. Hood of Tompion clock in raised position. Spoon locking device visible above case door opening.

16. (*Right*) Superlative year clock made by Thomas Tompion for William III, *c.* 1695. Royal Collection.

over the years. With the general introduction of bracket feet on late Stuart furniture, these feet appeared as well at the base of longcase clocks. A low plinth, which was shaped along the fronts and sides like an apron, was also employed to complete the design of the base.

As a result of the great interest in scientific matters which developed at the time of the Restoration, the Greenwich Observatory was established in 1675, with its famous Octagon Room designed by Sir Christopher Wren. The first Astronomer Royal was John

17. Clock Dial demonstrating Tompion's genius for perfect design, every detail being in the best possible taste. British Museum, London.

Flamsteed, whose tables of comparative solar and mean time (produced in 1666) and his tide tables for the Thames at London Bridge probably suggested the idea for equation and tidal dials on longcase clocks. Timekeeping of great accuracy was becoming more essential than ever. That outstanding maker, Thomas Tompion, was commissioned by Sir Jonas Moore to produce two clocks for Greenwich. These were to go for a year and were probably the first ever made. They had pendulums thirteen feet in length with a vibration of two seconds. It was originally intended that they should be wall clocks as the pendulums would not permit them to be placed in longcases, although one was modified years later, being fitted with a Royal pendulum and placed in a large oak longcase. It was acquired by the Earl of Leicester, but the second of these two remarkable clocks may be seen today in the Clock Gallery of the British Museum in London.

CHAPTER THREE

The Cushion Top Hood
(Late Stuart)

As the 17th century drew to its close, domestic interior design brought about an increase in the height of the main rooms of private houses both in the town and country. Ceilings of entrance halls, dining and withdrawing rooms became loftier and were sometimes decorated with high relief plaster work. Wall furniture like cabinets and bureaux also tended to be made higher, as were longcase clocks, although dials were still square in shape. To achieve this extra height hoods were built up with a succession of ogee and convex mouldings which earned the name of cushion tops. They were further embellished by pairs of gilded balls of turned wood or brass, mounted on small pedestals on either side, sometimes with a third ball finial in the centre, surmounting the cushion top. Elongated trunks, with these more elaborate hoods, now produced clocks well over seven feet, sometimes more than eight feet, in height.

Another change, c. 1700, was the substitution of hollow cavetto or concave mouldings beneath the hood in place of the convex shape to which reference has already been made. This alteration in a standard design was no doubt due to the shape of the heavier cushion tops, but it has always been a most useful factor in dating clocks made just before or after the turn of the century. Soon after the introduction of the longcase clock, small glazed windows appeared in the sides of the hood in order that the movement and the gut lines on the going and striking train barrels could be examined without removing the hood. These little side windows were for long considered to be a special feature of London-made clocks and therefore more desirable from a collector's point of view. However, it has been observed that hood windows have appeared in many provincial clocks of the early Georgian period. It was long accepted by many collectors, in the days when longcase clocks were more available, that a London-made clock was prefer-

18. (*Top*) Hollow or cavetto moulding beneath hood of Wright clock indicates post-1700 date of manufacture.

19. (*Above*) Smallwood clock showing windows in sides of hood proving this feature not exclusive to London clocks. (*See* p. 22).

20. (*Left*) Fine walnut veneered longcase, an eight-day clock with cushion-top hood by William Wright, Southwark, *c.* 1710.

able to any other in spite of the high quality of many provincial makers' work.

Another feature of hood design about this time was the introduction of a silk backed wooden fret in the frieze above the hood door. This enabled the sound of the bell striking the hours to be heard more clearly. Very occasionally, and only on the best late Stuart clocks, the fret was made of gilded brass or ormolu.

Towards the end of the reign of William and Mary, the colourful all-over marquetry patterns were replaced by a much more subdued style, where birds and flowers in vases were exchanged for finer designs of small arabesques. Sometimes found in panels outlined with boxwood stringing, as were the earlier bird-and-flower patterns (but later in an all-over decoration), these complicated arrangements of arabesque shapes have given rise to the more colloquial description of 'seaweed marquetry'. This style, more in keeping with the good taste of the period, was to last well into the first half of the 18th century. As previously described in the manufacture of marquetry panels in Chapter Two, two or three sheets of different coloured veneers would give the same number of completed panels of marquetry. Where one panel would have lighter coloured arabesques on a darker background, so the second would have a darker colour on a lighter ground. The second panel was known to the longcase makers as the *'contre partie'*; very rarely two longcase clocks may be found in the same historic house or art museum with matching marquetry patterns, like the two longcase clocks by Peter King in the Lady Lever Art Gallery, Port Sunlight, Cheshire.

Changes were also taking place in the decoration of brass dials and clock hands. The first cast spandrels were designed in the shape of a winged cherub's head, a popular motif used in the decoration of Restoration furniture, silver and other forms of domestic art, and now being made more complicated by the addition of a background of fretted scrolling around the head and wings. Shortly before 1700, another popular motif appeared comprising two little naked boys or 'amorini' supporting a Royal crown. This device is also found carved on the top rails of walnut chair backs and generally on woodwork of the period. For a considerable time the amorini-and-crown design appeared along with the cherub-head spandrels. Early in the reign of Queen Anne, the last of the Stuart

21. (*Left*) Walnut longcase by John Northey, London, *c.* 1760, with late use of arabesque or 'sea-weed' marquetry decoration. The Lady Lever Art Gallery, Port Sunlight. 22. (*Right*) Black japanned longcase clock by John Cottrill, London, *c.* 1735. Base slightly cut down at later date.

monarchs, two more spandrel designs became popular. The first consisted of a bearded head with a turban, sometimes referred to as a rabbinical head, or the head of a native with a feathered headdress. In each instance the head was surrounded by a complicated pattern of gilded scrolling. The other design was for a maiden's head, also with a background of scrolling. The heads were all smaller and not in such sharp relief as the winged-cherub type, but these new patterns were to persist well into the Georgian period and long after the cherubs and the boys supporting crowns had vanished from the scene.

Hour hands were also to change their shape from a simple spade-like design to a more complicated leaf form. The pattern, in some cases, became rather large and involved, but by no means as exaggerated as the hour hands on Dutch longcase clocks of the same period. It is possible to see at this stage the beginning of altogether more intricate clock-hand designs which were going to develop still more as the 18th century progressed. Minute hands had initially been quite plain, shaped pointers, swelling slightly from the dial centre end and then diminishing in thickness towards the point. Now, the shape was to take the form of a simple, slim letter 's' for about a quarter of the hand's length from the collet and thereafter into the plain, thin pointer as before. This 's'-shape, apart from a slightly more elaborate curvature, was to remain much the same for a number of years.

Casework was to continue to be made and finished in walnut and other fruit-wood veneers like cherry and mulberry well into the 18th century and for less important clocks solid wainscot oak was employed; but shortly a new and more colourful form of decoration was to be introduced. From Elizabethan times, when they first appeared in England, the applied arts of India and China had proved to be a great fascination, probably because of their rarity and exotic appeal.

23. Dial of Windmills' clock with unusually large hour hand.

Lacquered cabinets and small boxes had a special attraction and such was the demand for these items that a form of imitation lacquer soon appeared on the market. In 1688, two London designers, John Stalker and George Parker, wrote a book entitled *A Treatise of Japaning and Varnishing, being a compleat Discovery of those Arts*. The material for real oriental lacquerwork was a gum obtained from the lac tree. After laborious and careful application in special atmospheric conditions the eastern craftsmen produced their durable and attractive finishes. Stalker and Parker proposed to achieve a similar result using only paint and varnish. They described how this was to be done in their book and also included copperplate engravings of Chinese subjects suitable for transfer to the pseudo lacquer-decorated furniture. This so-called Japanwork was deceptively like the real thing when new, but it proved not to have the lasting qualities of genuine lacquer, the varnished surface eventually breaking down after a number of years into a network of fine cracks like an old painting. Black japanning with gilded scenes of Chinese life and landscape in slight relief was the earliest and most popular version to appear, but red, blue and green colours were also used; like other furniture of the period, longcase clocks were given a similar finish.

It has been recorded that longcase makers would send the doors of clock cases to Canton, China in the ships of the East India Company, to be treated with real lacquer. When returned and hung, the rest of the clock case would be finished with japanning to match the door. This imitation lacquer continued to be produced right into the Victorian period, a lot of it by gifted amateurs, but japanned longcase clocks seldom date after the 1760s, by which time the enthusiasm for Chinoiserie had abated considerably.

It would appear that throughout history longcase clock owners were suspicious that other members of the family or the servants would be tempted to interfere with the movement or alter the hands. Accordingly, a bolt was placed inside the case, immediately above the trunk door opening so that when the trunk door was locked the bolt would be inaccessible. A wrought iron rectangular staple was then fitted to the inside of the lower framing of the hood door and this was arranged to pass through a narrow slot in the lower part of the dial surround or bezel. When the hood door was closed and the staple had passed through the slot, then the

24. Dial of Cottrill clock showing fine original hands with urn-and-flower spandrels.

vertical bolt inside the case could be pushed into position through the staple effectively locking both hood and door at the same time. Bolts were often made of metal, but occasionally of wood, and when the passage of time has caused the wooden bolt to deteriorate or break, the slide in which it moved can still be felt on examination. I once looked at an early walnut longcase clock belonging to a friend which had a metal bolt for locking the hood; as there was no trace of a slot in the dial frame or signs of holes inside the hood door where the staple should have been, it could only be surmised that the hood on this clock had been largely reconstructed.

Clockmakers had always been aware, particularly after the arrival of the longcase clock, that they were dealing with two sorts of time: mean and solar. Clocks were being made which, with the improvement brought about by the introduction of the long pendulum, were keeping quite accurate time, indicating two sets of twelve equal hours every day.

There was one other piece of simple apparatus, however, which was indispensable to a clock owner; this was a sundial. Clocks in

25. (*Left*) Red japanned clock by William Evill, Bath, *c.* 1760; hood with hollow pediment, windows and original finials. 26. (*Right*) Detail of fine red and gold japanning on Evill clock typical of current vogue for Chinoiserie.

the late 17th and early 18th centuries were few and far between; if a clock stopped for any reason how was the correct time to be known to set it right again? The nearest church clock could be many miles away. So, when a longcase clock was purchased a sundial had to be acquired as well, in order that it would always be possible to correct the clock by the sundial, sunshine being available. That is why a sundial should normally be found in a churchyard when there is a clock in the church tower.

There was only one difficulty about this arrangement, owing to the fact that the clock kept average or mean time, while the sundial recorded solar time. Because of the rotation of the earth and the consequent variations of the seasons, a sundial could be as much as fourteen minutes behind longcase clock mean time in February and sixteen minutes ahead in November. For one day only in four months of the year–April, June, September and December–did solar time and mean time concur. Hence it was necessary to have some type of key for converting solar time to correct mean time. This was one of the tasks to which John Flamsteed, the first Astronomer Royal, turned his mind. His resulting Equation Tables were reprinted on numerous occasions; it is still possible to find an engraved paper sheet carrying a table of dates and comparative times, pasted on the inside of the door of a longcase clock. Such an example used to exist inside a fine clock in the main hall of Chastleton House in the Cotswolds.

27. Clock with equation table in door and wheels and pinions made of wood by James Harrison, Barrow, c. 1728. Museum of the Worshipful Company of Clockmakers, Guildhall, London.

Some ingenious clockmakers endeavoured to do without the rather simple but effective reference to an equation table by fitting a carefully designed kidney-shaped cam to the movement of a clock so that the time equation could be recorded on a subsidiary dial on the main dial of the clock. An example of this type of equation dial was designed by Daniel Quare, an eminent London clockmaker, c. 1710. Another well-known maker, John Ellicott, who had many fine clocks to his credit, later designed a longcase clock with a large equation dial situated in the upper part of the case door, separate from the clock dial itself.

While it cannot be disputed that at the beginning of the 18th century the finest longcase clocks were being made in London, there was an ever increasing improvement in the standard of work produced by clockmakers in the provinces. Much of it was in emulation of their brothers of the Clockmakers' Company in London, but in a number of instances clockmakers, often in comparatively small country towns like Wigan and Ormskirk in Lancashire, began to organise themselves for the better reputation of their craft.

Over many years, the Court Leet, or manorial court, at Wigan controlled the numbers of tradesmen, including clockmakers, who worked in the town. By so doing, the Court saw to it that only properly trained craftsmen were allowed to exercise their skills and those who set up in business in defiance of the Court were fined at regular intervals until they desisted. Some clockmakers, like Laurence Leicester, who was making clocks before 1710, were not easily brought to heel. His trade must have been a lucrative one because he appeared to treat the Court Leet fines purely as unavoidable business expenses. In the event, it was the Court who gave way to Leicester and in 1707 he was elected a Freeman of Wigan to ply his trade unhindered.

Apart from making clocks and sometimes watches, local clockmakers usually enjoyed fairly regular employment, repairing and maintaining town and church turret clocks which they or their predecessors had supplied. Another worthy maker of Wigan was John Burges who ran his clockmaking workshop from 1710 until 1754. It is interesting to note that he and other provincial craftsmen were men of parts, as quite a number of the Wigan clockmakers of the Georgian period were also practising gunsmiths.

Probably the most famous among them was William Barker who became a Freeman in 1748 and continued to work until his death *c.* 1786. He is best remembered for a remarkable longcase clock, completed *c.* 1780, which has become famous as Barker's Horological masterpiece. The case was made of veneered mahogany and stood nine feet in height, but it was the ingenuity used in designing the many working parts which made it such an outstanding piece of craftsmanship. Apart from the usual hour and minute hands, a long and delicate third hand, turning from the centre of the dial, indicated the graduations of the Julian calendar which was in use before Britain's adoption of the Gregorian calendar in 1752; these indications were marked around the inside edge of the chapter ring and the hand took a year to complete its movement around the 365 days. The Gregorian calendar was marked around the outer chapter ring. The same hand indicated the change of date on both calendars.

Above the main dial was an equation scale which was operated by a kidney-shaped cam similar to that devised and used by the famous London maker, Daniel Quare. Above the equation table was a globular moon, and the times of high tide at London, Liverpool, Bristol and Hull could be read on another scale. A small gilded replica of the sun ascended and descended according to the correct times for sunrise and sunset each day. Maintaining power, which is explained in Chapter Ten, was also included in the design of this remarkable clock. As well as striking the hours, the quarters were sounded on a chime of seven bells. Although this clock has been in the possession of the Liverpool Museum for some years now, it is a matter of regret that it has apparently not been possible to place it on exhibition.

Helm of Ormskirk, known to have been in business in 1761, was another very clever and gifted maker who designed a longcase clock with a perpetual calendar. Again, by calculating the shape of a special cam to control the mechanism, he was able to make the calendar self-adjusting, irrespective of the number of days in the month and accounting for the extra February day each Leap Year.

CHAPTER FOUR

Introduction of the Arch Dial (George I)

THE ARCH DIAL seems to have first appeared on the longcase clocks made by that leader among the old clockmakers, Thomas Tompion. A clock by him in the Royal Collection, made *c.* 1695, has what might be described as a rudimentary arch to the dial. In the year 1709, the same maker delivered a longcase clock to the Pump Room at Bath and this too had an arch dial. It was a somewhat shallow arch, but larger than the previous one, and must have marked the beginning of a new fashion in longcase clock design. It should be noted that a pointed Gothic arch is sometimes found on smaller domestic wall clocks of a much earlier date, notably on the painted iron dials of a few German Gothic clocks of *c.* 1500.

Early forms of the arch dial continued to be rather shallow; some makers, apparently anxious to keep up with the times, and having been caught with a stock of square dials, added the arch to the dial as a separate piece with the aid of rivetted straps at the back. However, it was not long before one-piece arch dials began to appear in quantity, although the square dial did not disappear altogether by any means and was manufactured throughout the rest of the Georgian period. Most arch dials had what was known as a broken arch, the diameter of the arch being slightly less than the width of the dial, leaving a small shoulder of about one inch on either side. Full arch dials without shoulders are sometimes encountered; one example is known by Henry Hindley of York (1701–71), the longcase clock having a 'ting-tang' striking work as well.

As with so many aspects of longcase clock design, experts have debated the possible reasons why the arch dial was introduced in the first place. One argument maintained that, as clocks became more complicated in the design of the mechanism, clockmakers required more space on a dial for subsidiary dials and hands. It is more likely that, with the ever-increasing height of longcase clocks

28. (*Above*) Dial of very fine mahogany clock with equation table in arch; by George Graham, London, *c*. 1740, British Museum.

29. (*Right*) Month clock by famous maker, Charles Gretton, London, *c*. 1700, in fine walnut case decorated with marquetry.

and the rather top-heavy appearance of some cushion-top hoods, the increased elevation of a dial with an arch would give a much more improved aspect to the proportions of the longcase clock as a whole.

Famous makers like Graham and Windmills were among the many names which now appeared in these early arches. Cescinsky and Webster in their book *English Domestic Clocks*, first published in 1913, illustrate an arch dial on which the maker's name, Charles Gretton, is depicted three times; first the name is shown in the early manner along the lower edge of the dial as 'Charles Gretton, London'. Then it was engraved on the chapter ring simply as 'Charles Gretton' and finally in the arch on a slightly convex oval lozenge as 'Charles Gretton, London'. The arch on this particular

30. Gretton dial signed on base and chapter ring. Multiple signatures would appear characteristic of this maker. (*See* p. 39.)

dial had been added as a separate piece of brass, but to have the maker's name advertised three times was very unusual indeed. It would seem to indicate that at that fairly early date in the 18th century, *c.* 1720–25, dial parts were being ordered separately from an outside engraver, or were being engraved in the workshop by a staff engraver, so that stocks were always in hand. In this particular instance, the square dial with the name at the bottom was probably taken from old stock. The chapter ring with the name on either side of the figure 'VI' would be from later stock and the arch with the name on the lozenge must have come from a third and last batch; this must have been ordered from the engraver complete with name and ready to be added to existing square dials which either had or did not have the maker's name already showing. This is an interesting example of a measure of mass production, even in the first quarter of the 18th century.

With the exception of some of the more outstanding London makers, the arch was very often used merely to carry a small tablet bearing some admonitory sentiment like *'Tempus fugit'* (Time flies)—a motto used so often and over such a long period that the term can only be taken as a mark of a mediocre clock with little original thought on the part of the maker. 'Time is valuable' was another motto somewhat lacking in inventiveness. Other maxims have a flavour of the sententious like 'A man is yet Unborn that Duely Weighs an Hour' which appeared on a Wigan clock by Peter Fearnley *c.* 1780.

Among the many companionable traits of the longcase clock is the striking of the hours, the distant sound being a reassuring one to many people at night as they momentarily awake before turning over and dropping off to sleep again. On the other hand, to the sufferer from insomnia the telling of the hours in the night watches could become unbearable, so once again the ingenious clockmaker provided a solution by installing in the arch a 'Strike-Silent' hand. This could be turned to 'Silent' before retiring to bed to prevent the striking of the clock during the night hours. When reverting to 'Strike' on the following morning, the clock would take up again the correct sounding of the hours, an operation made possible by the invention of the rack-and-snail system of striking control (*see* Chapter Ten) in the late 17th century.

Probably one of the most popular ways of using the arch space was to install a lunar movement or changing moon. On a disc, toothed along the outer edge and operated by a trip mechanism, two similar images of the moon were painted usually with a background of the night sky. Occasionally, these were engraved on a silvered base. The two moons were essential, as only one appeared in the arch at a time and as the waning moon finally disappeared on the right a new moon would appear on the left. It was a simple, effective and fairly accurate mechanism. From the beginning of a new moon to the end of its last phase takes twenty-nine and a half days. Each group of five days, with a group of four and a half days at the end, was painted on a scale around the outer rim of the lunar disc. This was done twice, once for each moon. As the disc rotated imperceptibly from left to right, moving slightly twice in twenty-four hours, the new moon slowly rose until it attained full moon status after fourteen and three-quarter days. The number of days was indicated by a fixed pointer at the top of the arch and as the moon began to wane it finally disappeared after twenty-nine and a half days.

One type of lunar movement was designed to emulate the true appearance of the moon in the heavens. Instead of a painted moon on a flat disc, a small sphere was placed in the arch so that it turned on a spindle. Half of the sphere was silvered and the other half painted black or deep blue. The spindle was connected to the clock movement so that it would make a complete revolution in twenty-nine and a half days, presenting to view the complete silver side of the sphere at the time of the full moon. This device is usually referred to as a globular or rotating moon and is so rare that a longcase clock equipped with it in the arch may be regarded as a clockmaker's masterpiece.

Square dial clocks were also sometimes equipped with diminu-

31. (*Left*) Dial of Lawson clock showing large minute numerals and rococo scrolling pattern spandrels, *c.* 1770. 32. (*Right*) Graduated scale in arch of Clare clock – similar to tidal dial – indicates moon's rising and setting. The Lady Lever Art Gallery, Port Sunlight.

tive lunar movements set above the dial centre where a seconds subsidiary dial would normally be found. Often a feature of north-country clocks produced in the late Georgian period, it was known colloquially as a 'halfpenny moon' because it was little bigger in size than that coin. It consisted of a small circular hole about $1\frac{1}{4}$–$1\frac{1}{2}$ inches in diameter behind which a toothed disc revolved, much in the same way as the larger lunar movement in an arch dial. Four small moons were painted on the disc, each appearing in turn at the opening. These consisted of a silvered smiling face representing a full moon; a scowling black face for the period when there was no moon and the two faces in between, painted half black and half silver which were intended to portray the first and third quarters of the moon's phase. The 'halfpenny moon' could not have been of any great information value because of the lack of any graduations indicating the moon's changes in days. A larger lunar movement in the arch would have been more useful.

Lunar movements were not merely toys, but served a useful purpose in the Georgian home. As no street lighting was available in the 18th century it was essential that social outings at night were arranged when the moon would be full or nearly so. Even on a cloudy night a full moon would provide sufficient light through the cloud cover to see by. Some years ago I was shown an 18th-century advertisement for a social evening at an inn at Hampstead. After listing the programme and the names of the artists appearing, the broadsheet ended with the phrase in quite large black print: 'There will be moonlight.' This must have been a necessary assurance to those who were going to venture out on the Heath, an area known to be frequented by footpads and highwaymen. To the farmer as well, a lunar movement was a necessity; the full moon within a fortnight of September 22nd or 23rd was known in the country as the 'Harvest Moon'. In a year of bumper crops it was essential to toil well after the sun had set in order to get the harvest home. A month later another large and usually brilliant full moon was known as the 'Hunter's Moon' because of the light it afforded the poacher by night. Mottoes sometimes referred to the phases of the moon. A somewhat obvious, but not entirely accurate, inscription around a band enclosing a lunar movement on a clock by Stephen Nelson of Wigan c. 1780, stated 'The Moon's Appointed for Seasons'.

Because of the connection between tides and the moon's phases, it was a simple matter to extend the working of a lunar movement to include a forecast of tide times as well. Tidal dials are easily distinguished, as two groups of twelve hours each in small Roman numerals were engraved or painted on a narrow band outside the scale of the twenty-nine and a half days of the moon's age. The times of the high and low tides indicated each day were correct to within half an hour and the spring tides, the highest tides, which occur shortly after the new and full moons each month, were also sometimes shown. Along with these the neap tides, when the high-water level was at its lowest, occurring soon after the moon's first and third quarters, were indicated. A provincial maker, William Bothamley of Kirton, produced a longcase clock in 1757 on the tidal dial of which he recorded the title, 'The Influence of the Moon on the Waters'. These tidal dials were a very real help to a number of people whose living had to do with the sea and wide river estuaries. Sea captains who otherwise might have missed the tide for their departure must have often consulted a longcase clock with a tidal dial in the public room of some quayside inn.

Another class of men who could also glean valuable information from a tidal dial were the drovers. In the 17th and 18th centuries large herds of cattle were often driven long distances to provide meat for the larger towns and cities. Where a drover had to take his herd across a river estuary which lay in his way, it was essential that he should know the time of the slack or low tide so that he could safely get his cattle across. This is the meaning of the term 'Drover's Wash' which sometimes appears on a tidal dial. The words 'Good Riding' also indicate when it would be safe for horsemen to cross a sandy bay or take a short cut along a shore line.

In the days before railways, hazardous journeys were performed by travellers in many parts of the country where a crossing of a tidal estuary had to be negotiated to save a long detour by road. Such a one was the way over the sands of Morecambe Bay from Hest Bank, north of Lancaster. In a large upper room at the inn there, where the party of travellers used to gather in wait for their guide, a large lantern used to hang from the ceiling, the light of which could be seen far across the sands at night. David Cox, the well-known early 19th-century watercolourist dramatised the scene in a number of his paintings with the guide on his white

33. (*Left*) Musical clock by John Ellicott, London, *c.* 1760; coloured prints applied to case door. The Lady Lever Art Gallery, Port Sunlight.

34. (*Top*) Dial of William Evill clock; rocking ship in the arch actuated by movement of pendulum. (*See* p. 34).

35. (*Above*) Indicator in arch of Ellicott dial selects numbered tunes, 1–18, listed inside case door. The Lady Lever Art Gallery, Port Sunlight.

horse and with his horn to keep the party together should the mist come down. No doubt there must have been a longcase clock with a tidal dial in that same inn, perhaps by William Parkinson who was making such clocks in Lancaster *c.* 1770.

Some tidal dials had a fixed indicator to point out the times of the tides and these were calculated for use at one place only. Other tidal dials are found with an adjustable hand which can be set for any port or estuary in the country, like that on a longcase clock by William Parkinson, which the author used to possess. To adjust the hand was a simple matter after the tide tables issued by the local port authority had been consulted.

Later in the Georgian period there appeared to be a demand for simple automata or little moving figures which were placed in the arch of the dial. Connected to the pendulum they rocked to and fro as the pendulum swung. A popular subject was a figure of 'Father Time' with his scythe, endlessly swaying as the hours passed by. The 'Rocking Ship' or boat was another fairly common toy; some very late clocks had crouching dogs or cats in the arch whose eyes moved from side to side with the motion of the pendulum, producing a rather disturbing and hypnotic effect on the onlooker. The rolling-eye type of automata are usually found in country-made clocks of the simpler kind with white dials and indicate a marked falling away in the standards of the professional clock-maker's usual good taste. Some early Victorian longcase clocks had miniature craftsmen working in the arch, one example being that of a joiner at his bench whose arms and body moved with the pendulum as he went through the motions of planing a piece of wood.

Yet another use for the arch dial was to position an adjustable hand on a musical clock which could be moved to select a tune to be played on the hour. The titles of a number of popular airs like anthems, minuets, jigs, and so on were engraved on a silvered tablet in the arch; alternatively just the numbers and a corresponding list of the names of the tunes engraved on a metal plate would be fixed to the inside of the case door for easy reference.

The introduction of the arch dial was to give rise to a new design for the longcase clock hood, which has been described as the domed top. It was similar to the broken arch top, to be developed much later in the century, but the arch was shallower and con-

36. (*Left*) Tall, slim mahogany clock by
Edward Tutet, working in London before
1754; member of Clockmakers' Company,
1765.

37. (*Above*) Mahogany dome-top hood of
Tutet clock; dial and fine hands indicative of
high standard workmanship.

siderably heavier in appearance than its successor. The arch or
dome consisted of multiple mouldings and was, in effect, of that
same school of design which resulted in the twin dome tops found
on Queen Anne cabinets at a slightly earlier date. Sometimes the
dome on the clock hood was surmounted by a rectangular box
shape or with a cushion top of the same form as that used on square
dial clocks late in the reign of William and Mary.

CHAPTER FIVE

An Assortment of Pediments (George II)

THE SECOND QUARTER of the 18th century in Georgian England was notable for the further development of two very different architectural styles: baroque and rococo. The baroque influence had come originally from Italy and France a hundred years earlier, the great ducal palaces of Blenheim in Oxfordshire and Castle Howard in Yorkshire both being magnificent examples of this fashion. Longcase clocks of the late Stuart period were also designed in this style, the spiral-twist pillars on the hood doors being typical. The emphasis in this vogue for baroque was primarily on impressiveness, symmetry and, to a certain degree, pomposity; this is where the tall, cushion-topped longcase clocks with their arch dials were in accord with prevailing taste.

William Kent was one of the leading figures in the sphere of fine and decorative art of this period from *c.* 1725 until his death in 1748. He was a well known architect under the patronage of Lord Burlington and was also an outstanding exponent as a landscape gardener, interior decorator, furniture designer and artist. He was largely responsible for the development of the Palladian school of architecture in England with its stress on classical and Italianate characteristics. Although the Palladians based the designs of their buildings on ancient Roman and Italian Renaissance models, they had little idea as to how the interiors of ancient homes had been planned or furnished. Accordingly, much of the furniture of the Palladian period was given definite architectural features, including pediments and pilasters on bookcases and cabinets. To give more interest, the apex of the pediment triangle was remodelled by removing part of the upper centre moulding and occupying the hollow space with a small pedestal and an urn or classical bust. This was known as the broken pediment, a feature which was also to appear on longcase clock hoods in a diminished size. A variation of the broken pediment was the so-called 'swan-neck' where two

38. (*Left*) Smaller than usual late-18th-century longcase clock; by James Binch, Liverpool, 1777–81.

39. (*Above*) Construction of Binch clock, including dovetailing on hood top, suggests considerable casework restoration at later date.

matching, 's'-scrolled pieces replaced the straight edges of the pediment moulding. This was a shape easily adapted for the design of clock hood tops and was to last right into the 19th century, though later in a rather debased form.

A new type of wood for furniture making, hard, heavy and even-grained with a deep red wine colour and moreover enjoying a freedom from attack by wood worm, had been making an appearance in Europe since the beginning of the Georgian period. The first shipments came from the island of Cuba and the timber was known as Cuban mahogany. Regrettably, an import duty levied in England prevented its general use at first, but, when the tax was lifted in 1721, mahogany was brought to Britain in ever-increasing

40. (*Left*) Good example of a painted dial north-country clock early 19th-century period; by Harrison, Ormskirk. 41. (*Right*) Elegant mahogany clock with early-type hollow pediment hood; by Robert Sanderson, London, member of Clockmakers' Company, 1731.

quantities, so much so that by the middle of the 18th century the supplies from Cuba had almost become exhausted. A slightly different variety of mahogany, lighter in weight and colour but providing wider boards as the trees were larger, was then brought from the Honduras on the Central American mainland. Another desirable feature of mahogany was that the material was capable of being carved to a pleasing effect, the result being clean, crisp and not easily worn. Because of the popularity of this carved decoration and to give full reign to the natural beauty of the new wood, marquetry was virtually to disappear for the next thirty years or so until its revival in the Adam period.

Furniture designers of the time now turned their attention to the fresh possibilities offered by mahogany. Probably the most notable among the books on furniture design was Thomas Chippendale's *The Gentleman and Cabinet-Maker's Director* published in 1754, which contained a number of designs for longcase clocks. These, however, were so elaborately decorated as to be impracticable and it is doubtful whether the patterns were ever actually produced. Although one particular design did not actually appear in the *Director* and cannot be credited to the famous cabinet-maker, a popular version of a longcase clock in mahogany did become known as a 'Chippendale Case'. It was usually decorated with a

42. (*Left*) Carved mahogany longcase clock; by Jeremiah Standring, Bolton, *c.* 1780; an unusaully fine case for a provincial clock. The Lady Lever Art Gallery, Port Sunlight.

43. (*Below*) 'Quoining' or brickwork on base of Standring clock, a popular decorative feature on north-country clocks. The Lady Lever Art Gallery, Port Sunlight.

swan-neck pediment and included an arch dial. Double free-standing pillars were frequently sited at either side of the hood door and blind frets, often of a lattice pattern, were added just beneath the cavetto moulding under the hood. Characteristic of this particular design was the occasional use of carved brickwork or quoining on the vertical corners of the base. Ogee-moulded feet completed this design which was mostly employed by provincial makers of the better type of longcase clock.

Chippendale's *Director* also included many ideas in connection with a new fashion which was to become exceedingly popular throughout Europe and flourished in England between 1750 and 1760. It became known as the rococo style because of the many natural forms originally used in the decorative motifs. These included rocks and shells which gave rise to the name rococo from the French words *'rocaille–cocaille'*. Rococo was a reaction to the previous fashionable style known as baroque and where the latter was inclined to a certain heaviness, using architectural features, balance and symmetry, rococo was lighter in concept, whimsical and asymmetrical in character. In Britain the new style was used almost entirely for interior decoration and for the applied arts. Probably its most important manifestation was in the popular vogue of the 1750s known as the 'Chinese Taste'. The use of japanning in imitation of oriental lacquer has already been referred to, but new furniture shapes were to be planned in a curiously outlandish fashion. These were admired by most people and accepted as oriental, but in effect quite European in origin. So many examples were given in the *Director* of 1754 for this new vogue that furniture designs adapted from it became known as 'Chinese Chippendale'.

As far as longcase clocks were concerned a new shape for the hood developed, which has been generally called the hollow pediment. Sometimes this has been called the 'pagoda top', although it is rather difficult to envisage where the resemblance arises. The two curved recesses on either side of the upper part of the hood, together with a slightly rounded top, bear little similarity to the roof of a Chinese pagoda or temple.

Throughout the latter part of the reign of George II many provincial clockmakers were earning a reputation for higher standards of craftsmanship and horological expertise. Family

44. (*Left*) Unusually tall 9-foot high mahogany clock with gilded decoration by Rollisson of Halton, *c.* 1775. The Lady Lever Art Gallery, Port Sunlight.

45. (*Above*) Hollow pediment; lack of quarter-hour marks and hands confirm date of Northey clock, *c.* 1760. (*See* p.30.) The Lady Lever Art Gallery, Port Sunlight.

firms were becoming established, like the Scholfields of Manchester, Salford and Rochdale. Major Scholfield was known to have been in business before 1730 and continued until his death in 1783; this firm continued to produce clocks until 1804. The Parkinsons of Lancaster were another family who made good quality longcase clocks, the first recorded member being Robert who was working in 1732 and died in 1760. William, his son, is listed as being a clockmaker in 1758. He in turn had a son, also named William, who was made a Freeman of Lancaster in 1789. Many provincial towns and cities alike were now providing opportunities for what was steadily becoming a nation-wide industry. Small communities with long histories, like Ormskirk and Prescot in Lancashire, were not only producing clocks, but were also making the tools and jigs with which the clockmakers in other areas made their clock parts. Chester, York, Edinburgh and Dublin, among others, had established associations of makers. While no evidence has yet been found of a Chester longcase clock being made before the end of the 17th century, John Buck of that city produced a brass lantern clock *c.* 1670.

Another worthwhile producer of longcase clocks was John Wyke (1720–87) of Liverpool and Prescot. He invented a wheel-cutting machine in the days when clockmakers were still making their own trains of wheels, eventually becoming so successful that he was able to build a fine town house in Liverpool which he called Wyke Court. It stood at the junction of Hatton Garden and Dale Street, but has long since disappeared; the Central Magistrates Court now occupies the site. Further research in the History Department of the local Picton Library brought to light a copper-plate engraving of John Wyke's house with an entrance for coaches through an archway into a courtyard. On one side stood the dwelling-house and on the other the workshop where John Wyke supervised the making of his clocks.

CHAPTER SIX

Advent of the White Dial (George III)

In the 1740s the art of enamelling on copper was developed at Battersea in London. A few years later the craft was further expanded at Bilston in Staffordshire and around the Birmingham area. The greater proportion of small antique decorative boxes and other personal trifles emanated from these places. White enamel on copper was obviously an attractive material for small clock and watch dials, offering the best possible clarity for telling the time. Unfortunately, enamel was liable to chip easily and clock dials were particularly vulnerable in the region of winding holes. Moreover, problems of manufacture made it extremely difficult to make an enamel dial large enough for a longcase clock. It is understood that such dials have been found but should be considered a great rarity.

This must have been considered a major setback, because clockmakers were certainly looking for a new type of dial, both for functional and economic reasons. Towards the end of the reign of George II longcase clock dials were certainly becoming difficult to read because of excessive engraved decoration and a multiplicity of hands. Apart from the usual hour and minute hands, the introduction of a long narrow, centre-second hand, sometimes referred to as a sweep, had been made possible by the use of Graham's deadbeat escapement. The centre-second hand was pivoted at the dial centre; because of its length and the normal recoil of the anchor type of escapement it had not been possible to bring it into use at an earlier date. The centre-second hand reached as far as the minute-mark band near the outer edge of the chapter ring, using the 60 minute graduations as seconds and making a subsidiary seconds dial unnecessary.

A further development in the operation of the dial calendar appeared about the middle of the 18th century when the thirty-one days of the month were engraved on the dial just within the inner

46. (*Left*) Multiplicity of hands on dial by Kirk of Stockport make time-reading difficult. The Lady Lever Art Gallery. 47. (*Right*) Detail of attractively painted dial of 'married' clock by Joseph Walker, Nantwich, 1781–95. The movement and appealing dial are not in their original case.

edge of the chapter ring. The date was indicated by a fine pointer, or calendar hand, also pivoted at the dial centre. This pointer was arranged to automatically record the change of date every twenty-four hours. The situation had now developed when four different hands were all operating from the dial centre and often against a background of an elaborately engraved dial. It was extremely difficult to tell the time correctly except by close examination of the positions of all the hands.

Some simplification of the longcase clock dial was imperative and a solution was achieved by making dials of iron, instead of brass, and painting them white. This was not only much more economical, but also gave greater clarity in reading the time. The centre calendar hand and the centre second sweep also tended to disappear, the old form of a subsidiary seconds dial reappearing together with another subsidiary dial of the same size which was used for the calendar. These two small dials were painted in immediately above and below the dial centre.

The painted iron dial is frequently discovered with a lunar movement in the arch, but smaller, square painted dials were also produced for thirty-hour country-made clocks. The cast brass spandrels were discarded as not being suitable for painted dials and also on the grounds of expense. Instead the corner spaces were filled with painted flower arrangements similar to those used to decorate the soft-paste English porcelain of the period. Chapter rings were also abolished as separate fittings and the hour and minute markings were painted in black on the white surface. Roman numerals continued to be used for the hours and the Arabic minute numerals also, at least until the end of the century, but only the 15, 30, 45 and 60 minute figures showed at the quarter hours and these, too, finally disappeared from most dials by the middle of the following century. About the year 1800, the use of vertical Arabic numerals instead of the traditional Roman type was adopted for the hours and although slow to supersede the latter, the former were to be employed extensively on mid-Victorian clock dials.

Changing fashion was to affect the design of clock hands as well, and early in the reign of George III the serpentine minute hand made an appearance. This was a generally popular innovation, particularly in the provinces and was used on painted and brass

48. Dial of Harrison clock with late-style hands and Arabic, instead of Roman, hour numerals. University of Liverpool.

dials alike. The London makers, however, seemed to prefer the straight and more refined traditional shape.

Although the painted dial was to be utilised to a very considerable extent and in spite of the fact that it afforded greater clarity for telling the time, it was still used mainly as a cheaper substitute for the brass dial. Accordingly, a similar version was provided by some London makers and those in the provinces who still preferred to adhere to the old, high standards of craftsmanship, in the form of a silvered all-over brass dial. Like its cheaper counterpart there were no attached brass spandrels, chapter ring or subsidiary dials; instead all these features were engraved rather than painted. Simplicity was everything in these silvered arch dials. It was an instance of a well-designed alternative and a fitting expression of the 'Age of Elegance', as the period has been termed.

Usually the arch contained a strike-silent hand, seconds and calendar subsidiary dials above and below the dial centre and flower groups or some similar decorative motifs engraved in the corner areas. It would be wrong to assume that the silvered all-over dial followed the appearance of the painted type as both seem to have been adopted at the same time. There can be little doubt, however, that the painted dial was inspired by the process of enamelling on copper.

Even if ousted to some extent by the new dials, the traditional pattern of brass dial with separately attached chapter ring and spandrels continued to be made. Three designs for cast spandrels are found on these brass dials during the period 1750 to 1800 approximately. One pattern was carried over from the later years of the reign of George II in the form of an indeterminate arrangement of rococo scrolling.

In the second type, occasionally found on dials from London longcase clocks, but more often on those of north-country makers, the four spandrels formed a set which represented the four seasons; although it has been stated that they derived from an early turret clock on a 17th-century church, the design was commonly employed by Dutch clockmakers and was probably copied from them. 'Spring' is depicted as a beautiful young girl with a basket full of flowers on her lap and holding a wreath of flowers in one hand; she usually appears in the top left corner of the dial. 'Summer', a slightly older woman with a suggestion of maturity, is in the upper

49. Break-arch mahogany hood with waved cresting, which encloses silvered all-over dial by Robson, Cripplegate, London, *c.* 1785.

right corner; she holds a sickle and carries a sheaf of corn. 'Autumn', in the lower right corner, is a young Bacchus with a wreath of vine leaves on his head, seated on a wine barrel, holding a wine cup in his hand. Finally, 'Winter' is portrayed in the last corner as a Chinese-like figure crouching against a stove for warmth. These spandrels are very attractive and once again demonstrate how the fashionable motifs of a particular decorative period were repeated in a number of different examples. For instance the 'Four Seasons' appeared as very appealing sets of small porcelain figures made at the Chelsea and Derby china factories during the third quarter of the 18th century.

The third spandrel pattern was a revival of the late Restoration period cherub's head, *c.* 1680–1700. It, like the 'Four Seasons' design, is found mostly on north-country clocks, but these cherubs' heads are larger than the earlier types and are frequently found to be roughly cast and rather poorly finished. There should be no difficulty in distinguishing them from the earlier versions.

Although the Adam period, which lasted from *c.* 1760 to 1790, has been referred to by furniture historians as the 'Age of Satinwood', longcase clocks made from this material are quite rare. The silk-like, golden character of satinwood proved to be an excellent ground for painted decoration and this has appeared occasionally on clock cases. A very delicate type of marquetry had also been revised for use on Adam furniture and this was sometimes employed on the doors of longcase clocks. Supplies of mahogany were plentiful and some walnut was still used, while country-made clocks were, for the most part, housed in oak cases.

About the middle of the 18th century, the process of cross-banding oak with walnut or mahogany became a widespread decorative feature in the northern counties, particularly in Lancashire and Cheshire. Cross-banding consisted of bordering doors and panels with a narrow border of veneer, set into the edge with the grain of the veneer at right angles to it. Following the appearance of the broken and swan-neck pediments, the earlier dome type still continued in use; but towards the beginning of the Sheraton period, at the end of the 18th century, it was replaced by a hood top, much simpler and lighter than the earlier domed arch, which became known as the 'break' or 'broken arch'. The new shape was used on narrow mahogany cases of medium height with chamfered or canted corners at the front of the case and hood. The architectural pillars at the sides of the hood door were done away with to accentuate the slim appearance of this new design. Polished brass balls with spires were placed on the steps formed by the broken arch to add a touch of brightness to the dark colour of the mahogany.

Thomas Sheraton, the well-known furniture designer of the late 18th century, included designs for longcase clocks in his *Cabinet-Maker's and Upholsterer's Drawing-Book*, published between 1791 and 1794. His suggested plans were impracticable, to say the least, and no examples of longcases can with any certainty be attributed to him. However, slim mahogany clocks with broken-arch hoods and a certain amount of yellow boxwood stringing, inlaid around the casework to form a contrast with the other darker wood, were very much in the style of Sheraton's period.

When the fashion of the 'Chinese Taste' was at its height in the 1750s, that famous dilettante, art lover and amateur designer, Horace Walpole, was strongly advocating Gothic forms of decoration as being infinitely preferable to Chinese. It is recorded that part of the library at his Gothic residence at Strawberry Hill near Richmond-upon-Thames, was modelled on the tomb of the Black Prince in Canterbury Cathedral, a notable example. The Gothic

50. (*Top*) Dial of clock by Lassell of Toxteth Park near Liverpool, *c.* 1770; with Four-Seasons type spandrels.

51. (*Above*) Third winding hole in chapter ring of Pace clock would suggest later addition of musical movement. The Lady Lever Art Gallery, Port Sunlight.

52. (*Right*) Veneered satinwood longcase with broken arch hood and Adam-style marquetry by Thomas Pace, London, *c.* 1790. The Lady Lever Art Gallery, Port Sunlight.

style proved even more enduring than the Chinese and was used
to a considerable extent in the decoration of late Georgian furniture. It appeared in the form of pointed arches for case and hood
doors together with pinnacles and clustered columns set in the
front corners of longcases and on either side of the hood door
openings. Many fine clocks were produced in these attractive
styles, mostly by London makers.

In the provinces the Industrial Revolution was bringing a new
moneyed class into being whose good taste was yet to be cultivated.
Taller, wider and mostly over-decorated clocks became the order
of the day, and brightly coloured, painted spandrels on the white

54. (*Left*) A good provincial specimen of an oak cross-banded longcase clock; by Lawson, Newton-le-Willows, *c.* 1775. 55. (*Right*) A revived Gothic style mahogany clock with painted dial; by P. Clare, Manchester, *c.* 1790. The Lady Lever Art Gallery, Port Sunlight.

dials with rubicund, smiling moons in the arches had a popular appeal.

Such was the growing demand for longcase clocks in the later 18th century that some form of mass production could no longer be delayed. A provincial clockmaker in the industrialised areas could order pre-fabricated parts from factories, and eventually complete movements, which only had to be put together. Dials, pendulums, hands, pulleys, bells, trains of wheels, in fact every part of the clock mechanism, could be ordered by the dozen or more.

Towards the end of this period a cast iron frame known as a false dial was introduced and used almost exclusively for clocks with painted dials. This enabled any shape or size of dial, so long as the winding holes were correctly positioned, to be fastened to any clock movement. This was done by attaching the pillars on the back of the dial to the false frame, which in turn was pinned to the movement. Although the majority of country makers were now becoming mere assemblers of parts, they still called themselves clockmakers; the more expert among them still knew how to design and make a clock in its entirety.

While the new clock-part factories springing up around Birmingham and in the Black Country could supply all that was required, distribution presented much more of a problem. The Duke of Bridgewater and prospering manufacturers like Josiah Wedgwood, were quick to see the advantages of the transport of goods by water. A canal system linking the main towns and river estuaries offered a solution and this was eventually built. However, there were many parts of the country where towns were connected by roads which were little better than tracks. Railways were still more than fifty years away, so the packhorse trains and the slow moving stage-waggons were the only means of conveying the packets of clock parts to the small-town clockmaker in his isolation. In many rural areas today the old packhorse bridges with their narrow roadways, low parapets and supporting arches are picturesque relics of the commercial past.

A feature of the country clockmaker's business which is not generally appreciated is that he sold his clocks over quite a wide area around his place of work. He, himself, would often transport a newly purchased clock a considerable distance in order to set it up. He also advertised when he would be in attendance at the inn or some other suitable rendezvous in a particular town or village on certain regular dates to take orders, carry out running repairs and generally maintain his customers' clocks. In 1745, the year of the second Jacobite rebellion, Henry Hindley of York, a very good clockmaker, had to furnish the authorities with details of his normal movements. This occurred because he was a known sympathiser with the Jacobite cause and a supporter of Bonnie Prince Charlie. For a while he was forbidden to journey more than a limited distance from York; in that troubled year Hindley's clock business must have suffered a serious setback. In the Castle Museum at York today there is a replica of Hindley's clock shop with some of his clocks in it.

CHAPTER SEVEN

Regency and Victorian Styles

WHEN THE Prince of Wales became Regent in 1810 (to 1820), following the illness of his father, George III, the event gave its name to a new fashion in the fine and decorative arts which was developing at the time. The Regency itself lasted just ten years, but it has been accepted by art historians and collectors alike that the new vogue continued into the early years of Queen Victoria's reign (which began in 1837) fading out *c*. 1840. It was an era influenced by the French Empire style to a considerable extent with rosewood and mahogany being the more popular woods for making furniture. Decoration was applied as an inlay of brass frets cut in architectural motifs like the anthemion or honeysuckle flower; brass and ebony stringing were also used, the latter on mahogany. The general characteristics of the fashion of the period was in the neo-classical style with overtones harking back to the Gothic and Chinese tastes of the previous fifty years. Thomas Hope, a rich young member of a banking family, who had been on the Grand Tour himself and was a practising architect and furniture designer, did much to foster good design in the Regency period.

An unusual kind of longcase clock known as a regulator now appeared in ever increasing numbers. Isolated examples of longcase regulators had, in fact, been made much earlier in the 18th century when progress in astronomical, geographical and geological matters called for still higher standards in accurate time-keeping. John Shelton, a reputable London maker with considerable experience in designing and making astronomical clocks, had been commissioned to provide a clock for the Greenwich Observatory. Soon after 1760, he planned a regulator clock for the Royal Society where it was employed for astronomical observations and experiments in gravitation. These were carried out in many distant places, as far apart as St Helena, the Cape of Good Hope, Barbados and Pennsylvania in America. This particular longcase regulator

56. (*Left*) Compensating mercury pendulum of Benson regulator. This clock is capable of extremely exact time-keeping. 57. (*Right*) Mahogany regulator longcase with mercury compensating pendulum by Benson, London, *c.* 1850. Benson was clockmaker to Queen Victoria.

was provided with a special container to protect it on its travels.

Shelton had worked for a while with George Graham, one of the most ingenious and capable of clockmakers. Graham had invented the mercury compensated pendulum in order to achieve as near perfect time-keeping as possible. For this contrivance, a glass container of mercury replaced the usual lead bob. The different coefficient of expansion of the mercury under changes of temperature counteracted the expansion or contraction of the iron pendulum rod, thus cancelling out any effect of the pendulum's vibration on

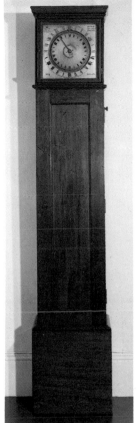 

58. (*Left*) Guardian watchman's longcase clock in mahogany case; made by Benjamin Vulliamy for the Public Record Office, dated 1843. British Museum, London. 59. (*Right*) Example of an early 19th-century case with a 'rabbit hutch' door.

the time. Other outstanding 18th-century makers, like Harrison and Ellicott, had also contributed to regulator clock design. These regulators were normally commissioned for special purposes; probably the increasing concern for thoroughness in business methods and for punctuality, coupled with an appreciation for fine workmanship, created the demand for good regulator clocks.

Early regulators had square, silvered all-over, engraved dials, circular dials appearing *c*. 1790. The dial lay-out for all these clocks was basically the same. A long minute hand of simple shape was pivoted at the dial centre with smaller subsidiary dials for the hours and seconds. This provided for greater accuracy in reading the time during scientific experiments or when the regulator was used as a master clock in a clockmaker's workshop. Cases were generally made of mahogany with a minimum of decoration, but some were veneered with rosewood and inlaid with brass in the Regency fashion. Occasionally, regulators are found in satinwood cases as well, although for the most part the emphasis was on quiet and sombre efficiency.

This type of clock was manufactured during the whole of the 19th century; in later Victorian times regulators appeared in slightly shorter walnut cases with semi-circular tops. Occasionally, these were enlivened with small wooden decorative frets placed just under the arch. Cases were normally fitted with plain rectangular doors where matching veneer was seen to advantage; later clocks had glazed doors so that the brass-encased weights and compensated pendulum could be observed.

A number of longcase clocks, similar in appearance to regulators, were produced for use in business houses and offices. Dignified and attractive to look at, they were very well made, but not as advanced in their design as true regulators. With painted dials, the hour and minute hands, unlike those on a regulator, pivoted from the dial centre. Those with arch dials had a strike-silent control at the top of the dial with the usual subsidiary dials below. Plain, spear-point hands indicated the time. Window openings were still provided in the hood sides of these clocks; however, where a striking mechanism was included, small panels of gilded, fretted brass of a simple scale design were fitted with a silk backing instead of glass.

Another version of the longcase clock also appeared about this time in the form of a long wall clock for use in public places like railway waiting-rooms. It had a circular dial with a wood surround and a circular glazed door instead of the more usual hood. A long door in the case revealed the usual Royal pendulum and weights; the trunk was rounded off at the base.

The gathering momentum of the Industrial Revolution in the early 19th century called for clocks which would check the arrival of workers at the factory and also record the patrol of the watchman as he made his rounds at night. While these clocks have little to commend them aesthetically, they were, nevertheless, ingenious mechanisms and a number of renowned makers like B. L. Vulliamy of London and Robert Roskell of Liverpool turned their attention to producing them.

Regrettably, the longcase clock was now to enter a period of decline and by the middle of Victoria's reign very few were being made. How this came about is difficult to understand because there had been a boom in longcase clock manufacture during the first half of the 19th century. However, a sad falling away in standards of good design became apparent. Cases were taller and wider with dials often as much as fourteen inches in width. Hoods were huge with badly shaped swan-neck pediments; the architecturally correct, fluted columns of the previous century gave place to turned spindles, sometimes incongruously topped with gilded Corinthian capitals. By now brass dials had virtually disappeared although the remaining painted ones were often historically interesting. Sometimes, instead of lunar movements, which still remained popular, scenes of local interest would be painted in the arch and spandrel areas. These were often quite well done, reflecting the popular art of the time when the cabins of canal longboats were decorated in the 'castles and roses' tradition. Topical events were also commemorated. The inscription painted on the dial of a Wigan clock, which may have been made shortly after the Battle of Trafalgar in 1805, read 'Sacred to Nelson'; however, the memory of that great victory must have lingered on in the public imagination for a number of years, so the clock may well have been of later date. Wellington and Waterloo have also been noted with pyramids of cannonballs, flags, muskets and guns all included in the painted decoration of the dial.

Makers' names and places of business were still recorded on dials at this time, but the majority of so-called clockmakers were in effect merely retailers of wares which they obtained from a wholesale trader. In a recent study about one hundred different makers' names were found on the dials of longcase clocks still in use on one of the Channel Islands, but only one had been made by a true clockmaker. The trunks of longcase clocks tended to become much shorter with correspondingly higher bases. Case doors were also reduced in size so that in some instances they appeared to be almost square and have been likened to 'rabbit-hutch doors'. These excessively large clocks with their brash, over-decorated cases seem to have grown in size, like dinosaurs, only to disappear.

Possibly the deterioration in the fortunes of the longcase clock was brought about by the flood of cheap Continental and American clocks which was pouring into Britain from the middle of the 19th century onwards. Although mostly mantel or wall clocks, they seem to have put paid almost completely to the longcase clock. It must be said, nevertheless, that many people who are not too worried about horological excellence find that these large longcase clocks have a certain antique appeal about them.

The making of longcase clocks did not come to an end entirely and special orders still resulted in the occasional specimen of very high quality being produced. A number of family firms of reliable and skilful clockmakers continued in business from the 18th century until well into Victorian times. They included people like E. J. Dent (who made the 'Big Ben' clock for the Houses of Parliament tower) and J. B. Joyce of Whitchurch in Shropshire. Although placed in the category of provincial makers, this firm had a long history of clockmaking and in the 19th century distinguished itself as a supplier of reliable railway clocks for stations, ticket-offices and waiting-rooms, many of these being of the wall longcase type already described. This firm was finally closed down in 1963. Thwaites and Reed of London (now of Hastings) were another partnership of clockmakers who, apart from their normal output, dealt in partly mass-produced movements of high quality which other firms used in wall and bracket clocks. The majority of the firms mentioned were also engaged in the manufacture of marine chronometers and turret clocks for which there was a considerable demand throughout the 19th century. Although the craftsmen who made these clocks could no longer afford the time to indulge in the decorative enhancement of movement parts, as they had done in the past, the plain but excellent workmanship put into these clock movements surpassed earlier work.

In the Victorian period longcase clocks with glazed doors and tubular bell chimes appeared on the market. A choice of chimes was normally available, these being Westminster, Whittington and sometimes Cambridge. Some early examples, produced by the firm of J. J. Elliott of Croyden had an array of shining bell tubes, three brass weights, one for the going train, another for striking

 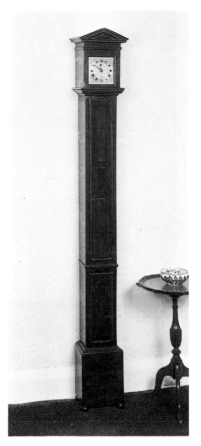

60. (*Left*) Electric longcase clock by Alexander Bain, *c.* 1845, pioneer in use of electricity to actuate clock movements. 61. (*Right*) Rare miniature longcase clock, 5 ft 11 ins high, in ebonised fruitwood case; by Samuel Knibb, London, *c.* 1670.

the hours and the third for the chimes, plus the large brass-covered pendulum bob–all visible through the glass door. This made for a confusing array of metalware which might better have been concealed. The design of many of the cases also left a lot to be desired.

Although traditional forms of hoods, with pediments, finials and bases with panels neatly bordered with moulding, sometimes conformed to the good taste of the previous Georgian period, too often longcases were overloaded with unnecessary decoration. Sad to say, there was a considerable demand for these clocks and they were not cheap. Many sold in the first quarter of the present century cost as much as half the price of a new, suburban, three-bedroom house at that time. However, they were well made and much of value was offered for the money, the more expensive models including a deadbeat escapement, maintaining power and a compensated pendulum.

During the 19th century, the principle of driving clocks by electricity resulted in the development of a number of longcase clocks, which were often like regulators in outward appearance. One of the pioneers in this particular horological field was Alexander Bain; he designed a number of electric longcase clocks in the 1850s, one of which in a Gothic-style oak case is illustrated. P. A. Bentley, an engineer who did much to develop electrically driven clocks, produced a number of longcases *c.* 1912. These were excellent in design and performance, and a number of them working on the earth-battery principle would run for many years without attention; there is an example of this type of clock in the Leicester Museum. During the 1920s some electric longcase clocks were imported from Germany. Without being in any way outstanding they marked, perhaps, a further step in this particular form of clock development.

'Grandmother' clocks have an attraction for most people as a more feminine counterpart of the larger 'grandfather'. However, their antecedants are very obscure, the majority of specimens being either highly suspect or modern productions. However, it is known that a small number of these diminutive longcase clocks were produced between 1660 and 1730, often by well-esteemed makers. They were less than five feet in height and had seven- or eight-inch square brass dials, conforming in every way to the style of their period, with ebonised, veneered, marquetry or japanned cases and with corresponding hood shapes. They are so rarely found that very few can have been made, yet they were not just whims of clockmakers with nothing better to do, but must have been made for specific reasons. In the late 17th and early 18th centuries many bedrooms and libraries in the larger houses had smaller rooms opening off, which were used either as dressing-rooms or private studies or writing-rooms. It could well have been that the little grandmother clocks were designed for this type of ante-room. It has also been noted that a number of these small clocks were

62. (*Left*) Attractive but faked 'grandmother' clock, skilfully reduced in height and width. The centre cut is discernible.

63. (*Above*) Original one-hand dial of faked grandmother clock, converted for use with two-hand movement.

equipped with alarm systems which would support the theory that they were designed for use in a bedroom. Because of this, the name 'boudoir' clock has been coined. Occasional specimens have cropped up, the characteristic features of which would indicate that grandmother clocks were made during all of the 18th century and into the 19th as well; but closer examination has revealed that quite a number of these have been altered in the past.

A fairly basic design for these small longcase clocks, with oak or mahogany woodwork, appeared in the early part of the present century. They were fitted with wire or rod gongs and spring-driven movements and are quite attractive little clocks; however many have that well worn tag, '*Tempus fugit*' in the arch and this somehow renders them commonplace. They turn up in sale rooms with engraved plaques attached below the hood showing that, in many instances, they were retirement presents of half a century ago. However, in these days of smaller halls in flats and modern houses these little clocks fit in very well.

CHAPTER EIGHT

Longcase Clocks from Abroad

DURING THE 18th and 19th centuries longcase clocks were produced in most European countries, including Holland, France,
Italy, Spain, Germany and some in Scandinavia. The American
Colonies, later to become the United States of America, also manufactured longcase clocks, where they were known as tall clocks.
Some were made in Canada as well. From the collector's point of
view it would be advisable to look for those clocks which have
found their way to this country in sufficient numbers to be considered as possible collector's items. Examples from Holland,
France and America are still to be encountered, although much
rarer than British clocks. Those from other countries are hardly
ever seen. A considerable export trade in English clocks has
developed over the years to most European countries and to
America; I have seen an English white dial longcase clock for sale
in an antique shop in Rome.

Dutch longcase clocks are likely to be more available than any
other European variety with the possible exception of those known
as French Comtoise clocks. Housed in walnut, marquetry or plain
oak cases, the national characteristics of Dutch clocks are un-
mistakable. It must be stressed here that Dutch marquetry seldom
equals in quality that found on English clocks. Although this form
of case decoration remained popular with the Dutch right into the
19th century, the standard of the marquetry cutter's work had by
then deteriorated considerably. Marquetry leaves, in bird-and-
flower patterns, often have blunt ends compared with the more
flowing curves of the earlier English counterpart.

The names of Dutch clockmakers are often met with in existing
records and a few are known to longcase clock collectors. Steven
Huygens, one of the more famous, worked in Rotterdam and
Amsterdam between 1697 and 1710. He was not related to Huygens, the mathematician, who earlier worked with Coster in

64. (*Left*) Early Dutch marquetry longcase clock by Jacob Hasius, Amsterdam, *c*. 1690. British Museum, London. 65. (*Right*) Decorative Dutch walnut longcase clock by Paul Braemar, Amsterdam, *c*. 1730. Dial has an arcaded minute band. Netherlands Clock Museum, Utrecht.

adapting the principle of the pendulum to clock movements. Steven Hoogendijk of Rotterdam was another noted clockmaker who worked through the greater part of the 18th century and produced many clocks. Jacob Hasius of Amsterdam was also a good maker of longcase clocks *c.* 1725.

Dutch clocks built in the early 18th century usually have arch dials with cushion-top hoods and a small, carved wooden figure of 'Atlas' carrying the 'Globe' on his back on the hood top is almost invariably indicative of a Netherlands clock. This decorative motif was used on Dutch wall clocks as well.

Another distinctive Dutch characteristic on many dials is the engraving of an arcaded minute band on the chapter ring which forms a series of small arches above and between the hour numerals. Not all Dutch clocks have this form of graduation and many dials are found to be very similar in design to those in British clocks. By the same token, the arcaded minute band is occasionally found on British dials.

The hands on Dutch clocks are normally more ornate than British versions of the same period. Hour hands are leaf-shaped almost as far as the dial centre and are decorated with very involved and delicate fretwork. That part of the hour hand which is pivoted at the dial centre is also often found to have fretted scrolling on it.

Moon discs are similar to those on British clocks, but are often engraved instead of being painted and the area surrounding the moon itself is frequently filled with a host of tiny stars. Spandrels tend to follow the same design as those on longcase clocks in Britain and the 'Four Seasons' pattern seems to have been a great favourite.

Early Dutch cases have a lenticle in the door, like their British counterparts, but a distinctive trait is shown in the base. This frequently has a 'bombé' shape, swelling into an attractive curved form like that appearing on other types of Dutch furniture, such as chests of drawers and bureaux. Alternatively, the base may have broad chamfered corners with a pronounced cavetto moulding at the bottom. Bun feet on longcase clocks lasted well into the 18th century. The similarity of the many characteristics described, illustrates the close links in clockmaking that existed between the two countries.

Longcase clocks in France, apart from the provincial types like

66. Dial of Rollisson clock (p.53) with later replacement hands and looped or arcaded Dutch influence minute band. The Lady Lever Art Gallery, Port Sunlight.

the Normande and the Comtoise, which will be mentioned later, appear to have been largely overshadowed by finely ornate table, bracket and cartel clocks (decorative wall clocks), upon which the 18th-century French clockmaker seemed to bestow all his talents. The longcase type of Paris clock, known as a *'pendule longue ligne'*, was often a magnificent creation. The *pendule longue ligne* usually followed the furniture styles of the time, the cases being veneered and magnificently decorated with quarterings of kingwood and tulipwood ornamented with ormolu mounts.

Toward the end of the reign of Louis XIV (1643–1715) Boulle decoration appeared, the invention of André Charles Boulle, one of the great French cabinetmakers or *'maitres ébénistes'*. He used tortoiseshell and ormolu, instead of various coloured wood veneers, to produce a delicate marquetry-like effect. Later, in the reign of Louis XVI, Boulle cases were produced in ebony and ormolu with dramatic effect.

Lenticles remained in vogue in France longer than in England. The fashion for large pendulum bobs with high relief decoration

77

67. (*Above*) Ormolu-
decorated French *régulateur
Régence* longcase with
enamelled dial by Le Roy,
Paris, *c.* 1750. Museé Arts
Décoratifs, Paris.

68. (*Right*) Elaborate
French pedestal longcase,
c. 1780. The case, by
Balthazar Lieutaud, Paris;
dial and movement by
Ferdinand Berthoud.
Wallace Collection,
London.

required glazed doors on the fronts of some French clocks, so that the decorative bobs could be viewed. Hoods became a special focus for decoration, often having quite large gilded figures of a winged 'Father Time' reclining on the top. True enamel dials, rather than painted ones, were introduced quite early in the reign of Louis XV (1715–74); because of the restriction on size imposed by the manufacturing process for enamel work, the dials of these longcase clocks remained comparatively small. This, however, was offset by the luxuriously decorated hoods. The hoods were made of gilded brass, decoratively pierced and fretted, and in keeping with the general elegance of the design.

A type of longcase clock which had a particular vogue in the great houses of France was the free-standing pedestal clock; a shape which enjoyed a special vogue was that of the gilded column surmounted by a dial which had a surround of gilded ormolu decoration instead of a hood. The weights descended inside the column and these were accessible through a cunningly concealed door. Later in the 18th century quite a number of '*pendules régulateurs*' appeared for use in offices, libraries and scientific establishments. The majority of these earlier French longcase clocks are very rare and fetch high prices when they appear.

However, towards the end of the 18th century a provincial clock was introduced which gained in lasting popularity. This was the Morez clock, produced in the small town of that name in the Morbier district of the Franche-Comté region of France. Because of the clock's association with these three connected localities it is variously known as a Morez, Morbier or Comtoise clock, the last being the more usual name applied to it. These are very satisfying clocks for a collector because of their several interesting peculiarities. Movements are mounted in a wrought iron frame and until quite late in the history of their production, had verge escapements. Anchor-type escapements indicate a fairly recent product. Comtoise clocks enjoyed an unusual distinction in that the hourly striking was repeated two minutes later thus providing confirmation of the time for those who had not heard it clearly on the first occasion. Circular enamel dials were set in square mounts of thin pressed ormolu which in turn was surmounted by a slim gilded metal cresting. Thin, flat steel pendulum rods were hinged at intervals so that they could be folded for ease in transport.

69. (*Left*) Repeat striking French Comtoise clock sometimes housed in bombé-waisted longcase with lenticle, *c.* 1825. 70. (*Right*) Japanned tall clock with domed arch hood, very English; by G. Brown, Boston, *c.* 1750–76. Greenfield Village and the Henry Ford Museum, Dearborn, Michigan.

Pendulum bobs were either of average longcase size very large and ornate with grid-iron type pendulum rods, more for appearance's sake than for temperature compensation. Comtoise clocks, especially those with the larger pendulum bobs, are sometimes found hanging as wall clocks, although many are contained in longcases of plain or painted oak and walnut. Because of the large pendulum bobs the cases are designed with bulging sides to accommodate the swing of the pendulum although the vibration is quite a small one. The hood with a glazed door encasing the rather small enamel dial and gilded metal surround, the swollen waist of the case with the lenticle in the door, and the very simple base all make for a slightly disproportionate appearance.

These clocks, however, are dearly loved by the provincial French and are sometimes seen among the furnishings of older type Parisian restaurants on Montmartre or in the side streets of the Left Bank. Comtoise clocks have so maintained their popularity that they are still in production today. Of all foreign clocks this is the one that is most likely to be met in the antique shops and auction rooms of Britain at this time.

Another form of French provincial longcase clock was known as the 'Normande' and as its name suggests was manufactured in the area of north-west France around Caen and Rouen in Normandy. Considerably over-decorated in a folk-art style, they varied quite a lot in shape. Some had rather unsightly expanded centre sections with disporportionately small hoods, while others, known as *'demoiselles'* for their feminine appearance, had slender waists. The majority had large lenticles in the case doors while the dials appeared to be on the small side; on closer inspection the dials are sometimes found to be attractively made of tin glazed pottery or Rouen faïence. These Normande clocks were eventually supplanted by the Comtoise longcases which seemed to have enjoyed a nationwide popularity.

In America longcase clocks were known as tall clocks and may be divided into three categories. The first included those made in the late 17th and 18th centuries by emigrant British clockmakers, who used the knowledge of clock construction and case design they had acquired in Britain. These clocks are identical to those produced in England during the early Georgian period and, being great rarities, are much sought after in the United States by American collectors. The chance of finding one that has been brought back to England is negligible. By the mid-18th century a second group had established itself—a number of very good American-born clockmakers. Included was the most famous of them all, David Rittenhouse, who worked in Norristown, Pennsylvania and later, between 1770 and 1777, Philadelphia. He must be considered the 'Thomas Tompion' of American clockmakers as far as collectors in the United States are concerned.

Thirdly, several generations of the Willard family produced good clockmakers, the most famous of whom were the three

71. (*Above*) American 'tall case' clock by
Frederick Wingate, Boston, 1804–35. Mabel
Brady Garvan Collection, Yale University Art
Gallery.

72. (*Right*) German longcase clock by J. W.
Wellershaus, *c*. 1840. Wuppertal Clock Museum.

brothers, Benjamin, Simon and Aaron. Simon became the best-
known of them all, although each of the brothers made some tall
clocks. Almost all of these clocks had painted dials, swan-neck
pediments and cases with high bases. Regrettably, most of these
clockmakers forsook the manufacture of tall clocks in favour of
the growing range of smaller wall, mantel and shelf clocks, on the
production of which the Americans were beginning to concentrate
all their energies.

73. Detail of hood, lunar movement dial and lack of proportion denote countrymade origin of Wellershaus clock. Wuppertal Clock Museum.

Another clockmaker who contributed in no small part to the history of American horology was Eli Terry. Born in 1772, he made clocks in the early part of the 19th century. In his younger days he made a number of tall clocks in the English Sheraton style, but he, too, eventually devoted all his attention to the production of the smaller clocks. The Terry family had a number of clock-makers among its members. Some of these later American tall clocks have found their way to England; while closely resembling the English product, they never seemed to achieve the gross proportions of some English north-country clocks of the Victorian period. Fretted wooden galleries were sometimes added to the arch tops of the American clocks which over the years have proved to be very fragile ornaments. Higher bases and rather delicate splayed feet usually call attention to their American origin.

German longcase clocks are seldom found in this country. Whether this is the result of two World Wars or for other reasons it is difficult to say. Occasionally, rare examples of country-made clocks do appear in rather quaintly carved and inlaid cases. The paucity of German longcase clocks compared with the plentiful examples of Black Forest wall and mantel clocks would suggest that very few of the longcase type were made for export.

CHAPTER NINE

Collecting Longcase Clocks

PEOPLE ACQUIRE longcase clocks in a number of ways and for a
variety of reasons. A clock that is an heirloom and has been
associated with the family for generations past should, of course,
be treasured and looked after. One of the best reasons for buying a
longcase clock is that it is such a likeable thing. Unfortunately for
the would-be collector, it has proved in recent years that longcase
clocks of all kinds have appreciated in value more than any other
form of antique. This has greatly puzzled dealers and auctioneers
alike because there seems to be no adequate explanation.

In the past, perhaps some people who would otherwise have
desired to purchase a longcase clock, were concerned about the
often very dusty mechanism under the hood and were not prepared
to involve themselves in possible future trouble. Certainly, many
antique dealers then, unless they enjoyed the services of a trusted
and competent clock repairer, would have nothing to do with
longcase clocks. Any which passed through their hands were
usually sold without any guarantee.

Purchasing a clock today might appear to be a little extravagant,
but there are few better forms of small capital investment than a
longcase clock bought at the right price. While its value appreciates
the dividend will be the enjoyment of its company.

Having acquired a longcase clock, it is important to become
familiar with its features. There are astonishing stories of people
not knowing anything about clocks they have lived with for many
years. After giving a lecture on antique clocks some time ago, a
member of the audience told me that there had been an old longcase
clock in their family for generations. I asked if it had a brass or
painted dial; after a little embarrassed silence the owner said that
she could not remember, although she had looked at it several
times a day to tell the time for many years. She also hadn't noticed
whether there was a name on the dial. It was a rather sad story of

84

someone living with a treasure and not realising it.

It is essential to learn some of the basic terminology that applies to clocks. The uninitiated refer to a clock face instead of a dial; to fingers instead of hands and to 'the works' instead of the movement. Perhaps this is being a little too punctilious but, like a good timekeeper, a clock collector should get things right.

Most longcase clocks strike the hours and, more rarely, the quarters also. Clocks that play a scale on a number of bells on the hour are referred to as chiming clocks, while a clock which will play a recognisable tune on the hour is known as a musical clock.

The owner of a longcase clock can spend many absorbing hours researching the antecedants of the maker. The London Clockmakers' Company and many other clockmakers' associations in the provinces ruled that their members should inscribe on the dial of every clock they made the name of the maker and the name of the town or borough where he worked. This was to ensure that any clockmaker could be traced in the event of unsatisfactory work-

74. Collier dial with revived pattern of cherub-head spandrels. The tune 'Charles' Dragoons' indicates Jacobite sympathies. (*See* p.86.)

75. Musical clock in
decorative inlaid and
cross-banded oak case by
Thomas Collier,
'Chapel-in-le-Frith',
c. 1750.

manship, rather in the manner of the Goldsmiths' Company, which
gave rise to the hallmarking of gold and silver.

Every clock enthusiast should own a copy of G. H. Baillie's
Watchmakers and Clockmakers of the World, which lists over 40,000
names. There are also many smaller books of a more specialised
nature which give greater details of clockmakers who have worked
in a particular county. Part of the enjoyment of owning a longcase
clock is knowing something of the man who made it; having completed your research it is useful to inscribe any known facts on a
small label, pasted on the inside of the trunk door.

It would be as well to appreciate that makers' names, engraved or
painted on the dial, were often spelt phonetically so that, for
example, Colson, Colston, Coleson or Coulson could all refer to the
same man. Baillie gives separate lists of several versions of the

same name. Whitaker's *British Books in Print*, available at most reference libraries, gives the titles of books on county clockmakers including those of Somerset, Lancashire, Westmorland and Cornwall. More detailed books of the makers of a particular town like Tiverton and Colchester are also listed. John Smith's *Old Scottish Clockmakers* gives considerable detail about makers, as does Dr I. C. Peate's *Clock and Watchmakers in Wales*. Local reference libraries will provide the next step in the investigation, while those who live near large cities can follow up their enquiries through archives in muniment rooms and in the local history sections of the more extensive central libraries. Parish registers are also very useful sources of information.

Some years ago the author acquired an eight-day longcase clock with a brass dial; on the chapter ring was inscribed the name 'Lassell Park'. Baillie gave no clue to a maker of that name although he did mention two variations of the name, Parke and Parkes; there had been a Joseph Parke working in Liverpool between 1734 and 1766. Could Lassell Park have been a relation? Liverpool did seem to provide a lead and a visit to the Central Library there might furnish some clues. A helpful librarian in the local history section suggested working through a list of 18th-century tombstones in the area. It seemed to offer a fairly slight chance of anything coming up, but then a surprise! A record appeared in a file about a stone in the churchyard of the little Ancient Chapel of Toxteth. On it was inscribed the name of Thurston Lassell of Toxteth Park. This could very well be the clockmaker who was being sought. Lassell was a surname, not a Christian name, and Park was Toxteth Park, part of a district known as Dingle where the Ancient Chapel still stands. A telephone call to the vicar and a subsequent visit produced more information about Thurston Lassell. In 1774 he had been a churchwarden of the chapel and in that year considerable restoration of the early 17th-century Nonconformist meeting-house had taken place. All the churchwardens had made a contribution, according to their trade or profession, in money or in kind and Thurston Lassell had provided a large clock for the gallery in the church. Finally the vicar showed me Thurston's tombstone in the graveyard. The old Lancashire clockmaker had, literally, been run to earth at last.

A collector once wrote that he had traced the maker of one of his longcase clocks to a village not far from Windermere in the English Lake District. Having made his way to a cottage where the maker of his clock was reputed to have lived, he was shown a large stone outhouse which was thought to have been the workshop. Having been given permission to inspect the interior of the building he found that it was a typical Lakeland drystone and slate structure without plaster on the inside walls. To his great joy he discovered a considerable number of dusty old corroded clock wheels and other parts of clock movements in the spaces between the stones of the wall near a window. These must have been put there by the clock-maker all those years before as he replaced worn items in a clock on his workbench before the window. The name of the clockmaker was Jonas Barber of Winster whose career has been investigated and written up in recent years. He has been found to have been an extremely able maker and yet for a long time his work has been little known.

There must be many more excellent provincial makers whose work is waiting to be documented by enthusiastic collectors. Such links with the past are the essence of collecting longcase clocks.

The often itinerant nature of the old provincial clockmaker's work is sometimes the cause of mystification when longcase clock owners are trying to trace the origins of the makers of their clocks. The name of the maker might appear in one of the recognised lists of makers; however the place is not the same as that on the dial. This is because the name given need not necessarily have been that of the locality where the clock was actually made, but where it might have been sold. So, if a dial bears the name of a village ten or fifteen miles away from a larger town, where a recorded maker was known to have been producing clocks, there would be little doubt that this was the clockmaker being sought.

Decorative features and characteristics of certain periods which contribute to the appearance of a longcase clock will often enable its date of manufacture to be estimated approximately, often helping to date it within twenty years or so, one way or the other.

However, these characteristics are not always infallible, as some traditional forms and shapes were occasionally used by iso-lated, provincial makers long after they had become generally unfashionable in the more important towns and cities of the realm. Nevertheless, the collector of longcase clocks will find that a knowledge of proportion, shape and decorative detail on the hood, case and dial, and the design of the hands and spandrels can be invaluable in reaching a true estimate of the age of a clock.

Attempts to divide historical time into convenient sub-sections are always a matter of opinion. Periods overlap; chairmakers did not stop using Queen Anne legs for their chairs on the day she died. Although Queen Victoria came to the throne in 1837, Regency styles persisted for many years after, so that it is not always easy to say whether a piece of furniture is early Victorian or late Regency.

In order to give some idea of period styles and the dates when they were fashionable, a chart has been included. This enables one to associate dates with period characteristics, always remembering that these frequently derived from a previous period and often survived into a later one.

Some years ago I met a collector of longcase clocks who lived in a rather small house, but he had managed to fit into it about a dozen longcase clocks. He used to say that one day he was going to move to a bigger house and fill it full of clocks. This was over twenty years ago when longcase clocks were absurdly cheap and his ambition could quite easily have been achieved. He never seemed to notice his wife's face when he voiced his intention, or he would have appreciated that it was never going to be realised.

Clock collectors today are faced with the dual problems of scarcity and high cost; some might settle for one good clock with a fine dial, original hands and a beautifully veneered or marquetry case and made by a famous maker. This in itself, of course, would not be a collection, but it would be a collector's piece having all that was best in a particular period and would be a joy to live with.

It is still possible to purchase a new longcase clock, made in the traditional way. A specially commissioned one would cost a great deal of money, but some old established firms of repute hold stocks of good clocks which are probably less costly to buy than a second-rate old one.

Another suggestion would be to aim at gathering together a small collection of three clocks. The first should date from *c.* 1700 and should have a walnut case, an eight-day movement and a good square dial with all the early attributes such as an interesting chapter ring, fine hands and well-cast gilded spandrels. It should

	RESTORATION 1660–1690	LATE STUART 1690–1720
HOODS	* Pedimented tops with plain architectural pillars attached to doors. * Occasional gilded metal mounted ornaments. * Later door pillars in baroque spiral twist form with carved cresting on flat hood tops.	* Cushion tops now general with fluted pillars on some doors; turned and gilded balls an added ornament.
CASES	* Ebonised pine or ebony veneer. * Convex moulding under hood. * Ball feet or simple plinth on base * Walnut and other veneers replace ebonised wood * Bird-and-flower marquetry in panels * Small lenticle windows in many doors.	* Cases become taller * All-over marquetry changes to 'seaweed' type * Lenticles tend to go out of use * Shaped plinths or bracket feet employed on bases * Convex moulding under hood now replaced by cavetto or hollow shape
DIALS	* Brass * Narrow chapter ring with Arabic numerals inside minute band on two-hand clocks * One-hand clocks have quarter-hours only engraved on inside edge of ring (this hardly a recognition clue, as one-hand clocks were made well into second half of 18th century) * Dial centre simply matted * Well finished cherub-head spandrels * Spade-shaped hour hand; seconds hand without tail * Maker's name engraved along bottom edge of dial	* Brass * Minute numerals appear outside minute band * Chapter rings tend to widen as hour numerals become larger * Cherub spandrels superseded by putti supporting crown device * Hour hands become more leaf shaped * Square or round calendar apertures

	EARLY GEORGIAN 1720–1750	MID-GEORGIAN 1750–1770
HOODS	* Arch dials with double cushion tops increase height of clocks considerably. * Domed arch tops introduced to achieve better proportions.	* Pillars detached from door and positioned, free-standing at either side * Hollow pediment tops appear * Open frets used in decoration * Vogue for architectural broken pediments
CASES	* Rectangular case doors change to round or broken arch tops * Mahogany introduced, but walnut still used as well as oak for cheaper clocks * Japanned cases in black, red or green and gold now fashionable	* Blind frets in frieze under hood * Pointed Gothic arch shape used for some case doors * Quarter round fluted columns appear as canted corners; brickwork or quoining on base; ogee feet * Mahogany for the most part but oak continuing to be used in the provinces * Japanned pine cases remain popular; walnut still used occasionally
DIALS	* Brass * Arch dial introduced * Minute numerals steadily increase in size * Spandrels of maiden, rabbinical and savage head with feathered head-dress appear	* Quarter-hour markings no longer shown * Flower-and-shell and other spandrel patterns give way to rococo scrolling * Centre-seconds hands become common * Excessive engraved decoration on provincial clock dials, together with multiplicity of hands render time-telling difficult * Arc of circle calendar apertures introduced but square shapes also in use

	LATE GEORGIAN 1770–1810	REGENCY 1810–1840
HOODS	* Swan-neck pediments very popular * Pairs of fluted pillars at each side of some large mahogany clocks * Broken-arch tops appear later in period * Round or pedimented tops for regulators	* Revival of classical styles * Some Gothic decoration, e.g., clustered columns * Debased swan-neck pediments on many provincial clocks
CASES	* Simplicity of case design * Satinwood with delicate marquetry or painted decoration	* Rosewood or mahogany woodwork inlaid with brass or ebony stringing and other decorative motifs, like honeysuckle pattern
DIALS	* Painted white dials introduced * Engraved, silvered all-over dials without attached chapter rings and spandrels now used on more expensive clocks * Arabic minute numerals equal in size to Roman hour numerals produce effect of lack of proportion	* Arabic figures appear on some painted dials * Matching hour and minute hands in stamped brass replace steel types on white dial clocks

	EARLY VICTORIAN 1840–1860	LATE VICTORIAN 1860–1900
HOODS	* Earlier features persist, e.g., mahogany cross-banding on oak * Turned spindles used instead of pillars at hood sides present poor appearance	* Sometimes retain decorative characteristics of earlier styles but mostly exaggerated, e.g. domed and broken arch designs for hood tops. * Occasionally accurate reproductions of styles in fashion 100 years earlier were made.
CASES	* Case doors become much shorter * Proportions very large – almost elephantine on some provincial clocks * Mahogany and oak used extensively but rosewood veneer with brass stringing and some late Regency decorative motifs survive. Ebony stringing with mahogany veneer also persists after the Regency. Walnut re-introduced.	* Over-decoration in form of all-over carving to match that on hood was used. * Glazed doors on the trunk, often with astragals or glazing bars, were popular to display highly polished brass-covered weights and large pendulum bob. * Oak – often heavily carved with Neo-Gothic decoration – becomes more popular than mahogany; the latter still employed. Burr walnut used for veneering regulator cases.
DIALS	* Many late Georgian and Regency features still in use * Gongs tend to be substituted for bells in striking clocks	* Either painted or silvered all-over – occasionally with attached chapter ring but generally exceeding standards of good taste * Arabic numerals often used instead of Roman type, these being contained separately in circular or oval cartouches * Some lunar movements still included but sub-dials very popular for variety of purposes, e.g. to indicate choice of Cambridge or Whittington chimes.

76. (*Left*) Floral marquetry clock by Joseph Windmills, *c.* 1690. Absence of marquetry in base indicates some restoration.

77. (*Above*) Thirty-hour clock in stripped pine case by James Barfoot, Winbourn, *c.* 1775; original hood without pillars.

have a lenticle, too, and a cushion top on the hood and be not much above seven feet in height. The second clock should be representative of the mid-18th century. A smallish, country-made thirty-hour clock with a rope- or chain-drive would do very well. The brass dial should have good spandrels, perhaps a set of the 'Four Seasons' and again original hands. The case would be simple and made in pine or oak with cross-banding in walnut or mahogany. As this is to be an eclectic longcase-clock collection, small but representative, the third clock should date from *c.* 1800 and be in a slim, mahogany case. A painted, arch dial with a moon in it and late wrought steel or stamped brass hands of the period would be agreeable. A clock with a tidal dial would be a valuable acquisition for anyone living near the sea so that the time of high tide would always be known. Make sure before buying that everything is in working order.

A good longcase clock is a personality and should not be cramped for space. One clock in a room is sufficient, but take into consideration the availability in even a small house. Leaving out the bed-

78. (*Above*) Engraved river scene on Barfoot clock dial. Movement has four-days going duration with striking immobilised.

79. (*Right*) Mahogany longcase clock by Barraud, London, *c.* 1810. Case door in accord with revived Gothic fashion.

95

80. (*Left*) An attractive provincial clock in well-proportioned mahogany case by Benson, Whitehaven, *c.* 1775.

81. (*Above*) Dial of Benson clock with centre calendar hand and late 18th-century serpentine minute hand.

rooms, there is a place in the hall for a clock, and the dining-room, the sitting-room and the living-room could take one each. A turn on the stairs is a fine place for a clock, but be sure that it is fixed to the wall. One could also go on the upstairs landing. So there is room for six longcase clocks of one sort or another.

To the collection of three already described there would now be room for a little, one-handed clock with a brass dial in a slim country-case of oak. A good regulator would add tone in a horological sense, particularly one in a rosewood case with brass inlay and stringing. Finally, to complete the half dozen, a 'foreign gentleman' might be considered, either a 'Dutchman' or a 'Frenchman' or, perhaps, an antique grandmother clock. Concerning the latter, great care must be taken as very old grandmothers are not always what they seem—clockwise, that is.

I have met many collectors of longcase clocks in my travels, but I remember one especially—a knowledgeable and discriminating enthusiast of many years—who lived in a house in the country, with numerous spacious rooms. It was an ideal place for longcase clocks, as more than one in a room was hardly noticed. One stood in the wide hall, which had a black-and-white tiled floor, like a painting of a Dutch interior, completing a most beautiful scene. Only an honoured few were permitted to strike or there would have been pandemonium on the hour. The sound of all the clocks ticking away filled the house, but not obtrusively, perhaps like the comforting music of distant water running in a stream.

It might be said that because of the cost, not many people will be able to attempt the collections suggested. Well, there is always the 19th century. It is not the best period from which to choose a collection of longcase clocks, but they are still available from that era; a provincial white dial with an inlaid, colourful case and a lunar movement would give a lot of pleasure. For a second choice seek out a mid-Victorian office clock in a well proportioned mahogany case with restrained decoration. The old brass dials with detachable chapter rings and spandrels will not be available much longer at a reasonable price. However, a silvered all-over, engraved brass dial can be very attractive. Add to these a hanging, wall longcase in a Sheraton-style design or a French Comtoise clock in a simple oak or walnut bombé case and you would still be doing very well.

Some years ago I purchased a longcase clock in a public saleroom having been attracted to it by an apparent anomaly in its appearance. The clock was rather dilapidated and the case appeared to have been made of mahogany, but it had a lenticle in the door with a brass bezel or surround. Now, by the time clockmakers began to use mahogany for their casework, lenticles had become obsolete in the great majority of clocks. I examined the case more closely and to my great interest found that it was not mahogany, but had been coated with mahogany varnish. Faintly discernible under the varnish could be detected the quartered and cross-banded veneer

82. **A.** Typical longcase clock *c.* 1690;
a. fret in frieze for bell sound; b. brass
dial with attached Roman numeral
chapter ring, cast spandrels and square
date opening; c. convex moulding
under hood; d. half-round cross grain
beading surrounding trunk door; e.
glazed lenticle with half round wood or
brass surround; f. well proportioned
base with bun or low bracket feet or
shaped plinth; g. windows in hood
sides. Spiral twist columns on hood door;

B. High, wide longcase *c.* 1810; a.
swan neck pediment; b. lunar
movement; c. arched painted dial,
arabic numerals stamped brass hands,
arc of circle date opening; d. free-
standing spindle columns, cavetto or
hollow moulding under hood; e. short
'rabbit hutch' type door in trunk; f.
comparatively high base with
elongated bracket feet.

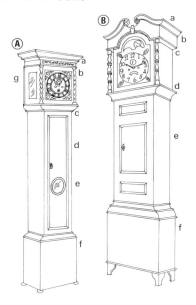

83. Development of hour- and minute-
hand styles between 1670 and 1800.

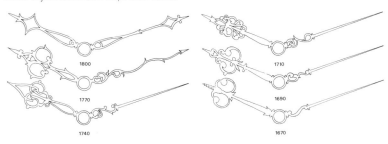

of a walnut clock. I bought the clock, very cheaply as it turned out,
and carried it off for restoration. The earlier wax polishing of the
case had prevented the varnish from penetrating the grain of the
walnut and I found that it was easily removed as age had rendered
it very dry. Eventually, a beautiful golden, burr-walnut case was
revealed which was quite in keeping with the lenticle. This is just
a little illustration of how period characteristics helped to uncover
what amounted to be a concealed treasure. One can only wonder
why the mahogany varnish had been applied in the first place.
Perhaps it was an instance of 'keeping up with the Jones's' when
mahogany was becoming the fashionable wood for furnishing,
early in the reign of George II.

98

CHAPTER TEN

The Movement

MANY PEOPLE WHO respond to the charm of longcase clocks are mystified by the fact that the movement, which may be 300 years old or more, still continues to go without, apparently, becoming worn out. This is a misleading idea which can best be compared with the story of the countryman who had a yard brush which he maintained had lasted all his life. Sometimes it had to have a new head and sometimes a new handle but it never wore out. Similarly, the movement of a clock, sometimes incorrectly called 'the works', will have had many of its working parts replaced over the years: new pinions will have been fitted where the leaves of the old ones have become worn; arbor holes will have been re-bushed where they have become too large causing excessive play or sideways movement in the wheel train, which in turn, will have prevented the toothed wheels engaging closely in the leaves of the pinions and the clock will have stopped; worn pallets on the escapement anchor will have been replaced from time to time or a new anchor fitted; and every few years the gut lines which carry the weights will have been renewed. When defects such as these occur they can be made good by a professional clock restorer who will make replicas of the damaged parts. This he will do by hand so that they match the original design of the maker.

In an age when little was known about scientific instrument-making or mechanical engineering, the clockmaker was 'ahead of his time'. The great pride he took in his work and the care with which he added small decorative details to those parts of the movement, which were not normally visible, indicate that he must have revelled in his work. Clockmakers were indeed perfectionists, this point being well illustrated by the introduction of maintaining power in longcase clocks. It is not always realised that when an eight-day clock, or one of longer duration, is wound up, the movement goes backwards during the operation. The action of winding

99

temporarily removes the driving force of the weight; the momentum of the pendulum, no longer activated by the movement, now takes over and causes the wheel train to operate in the reverse direction. This can be checked by observing the seconds hand as the clock is being wound, when it will be seen to be moving in an anticlockwise direction for a short time. Although the recorded time lost in this way was infinitesimal, nevertheless the dedicated clockmaker could not abide it, introducing the ingenious mechanism known as 'maintaining power' to remedy the small fault. Diminutive brass shutters were fitted behind the winding holes; before the winding key could be inserted the shutters had to be opened by pulling a cord line which hung inside the clock case. This action put a small spring into compression which took over the function of the weight while it was being wound up and so the clock was kept going forward. The action of the maintaining power lasted just long enough for the clock to be wound, not a second being lost in the process. The shutters would then return automatically to their original closed position ready for the next winding. It is interesting to note that the simpler mechanism of a thirty-hour clock has a built-in maintaining power. As the rope or chain is pulled to wind up the clock only the ratchet-controlled pulley which carries the chain is affected; although the weight is actually being lifted it still continues to operate the clock. This occurs because another loop of the chain passes over a fixed pulley which activates the wheel train.

The clockmaker's dream has always been to achieve perpetual motion in a clock. This ambition, like the search in the 18th century for the philosopher's stone which would transmute base metal into gold, was never to be realised. The most common going duration for a longcase clock was eight days, but some were designed which would go without winding for a month, three months or even a year.

A useful feature in helping to recognise a month clock is that the winding handle is turned in an anti-clockwise direction because of the extra wheel in the train which extends the going period. Year clocks were nearly always timepieces, that is, they didn't strike the hours, because all extra mechanisms such as striking trains, calendars, lunar movements and so on were usually eliminated to diminish friction as far as possible. However, a year clock with an

84. Large weights of
Gretton clock almost
filling the case indicate
going duration of one
month or more. (*See*
pp.39, 40.)

equation movement was made in the early 18th century by Daniel
Quare. The longer train of wheels and pinions and the very large
weight necessary to overcome the inertia of the movement were
all that were considered essential in the design of a clock with such
a long going period.

Two forms of striking mechanism are found in longcase clocks.
The earlier count-wheel type, normally used on thirty-hour clocks
and some eight-day movements, continued to be employed until
well into the 18th century. The count wheel may be recognised
either as a solid brass disc or a spoked wheel fitted on the square
of an arbor in the striking train. It has small slots cut out of the
circumference, the distance between each slot governing the
number of strokes of the bell hammer. The count wheel is sometimes found attached to the striking train barrel in eight-day clocks
while it is normally fitted separately to the backs of thirty-hour
movements. A defect in the count-wheel form of striking is that
it can easily go out of phase, that is, a clock might strike six times
at 4 o'clock and continue to be two hours out at every hour until
adjusted. The other is known as the rack-and-snail device, which
was invented by Edward Barlow *c.* 1676. Barlow was a mysterious
person, reputed to have been a secret Catholic priest although he

85. (*Left, top*) Eight-day movement of Barraud clock with 'rack and snail' striking control mechanism attached to hour wheel. (*See* p.95.)

86. (*Left, bottom*) Back view of Markwick arch dial *c.* 1725 showing arch attached with straps and count-wheel striking mechanism.

87. (*Above*) Walnut longcase by Thomas Tompion, *c.* 1686, with month movement and maintaining power shutters behind the winding holes.

was well known in the London of his day as an amateur clock designer. The rack was used to measure the number of strokes struck at the hour and the snail, a stepped cam attached to the hour wheel controlled that number. The rack-and-snail mechanism enabled repeat striking to be introduced. It is still employed on modern clocks today.

Returning the striking mechanism to the correct sequence is quite easily done. The first method takes a little longer, but can be done without removing the hood. Note the number of hours struck at any one time; then unhook the weight from the striking train, which is usually on the left. Carefully move the hands of the clock forward and you will hear a clicking sound each time the minute hand passes the 12 o'clock figure; the clock will not strike because the weight has been removed. When the hands are about 15 minutes short of the next hour beyond that which was previously sounded, hang the weight on its hook and move the hands forward to the hour when the correct number of strokes will be sounded on the bell. Now move the hands forward to the correct time, stopping at each hour to permit the clock to strike the correct number of hours in passing.

Another procedure, which is simpler, but requires the hood to be removed, entails depressing a small lever, which is found on an arbor just above the hammer tail on the left of the movement. Do not remove the weight of the striking train, but cause the clock to strike the full sequence each time by depressing the small lever. Continue to do this until the correct number of strokes on the bell is reached to coincide with the time shown by the hands. Frequently the clock gets out of phase with the striking when the hands are moved on after the clock has stopped without permitting the bell to be struck the correct number of times as the hands pass the hour. When the striking train weight is allowed to unwind to its full extent without the going train stopping, the clock will also get out of phase with the striking. The going train carries on, perhaps for another hour or two, without the clock striking.

The ornately turned brass pillars which separate the front and back plates of the clock movement are themselves often indicative of the quality of the workmanship. A provincial clock made in the 18th century would normally have four pillars, although earlier London clocks had five or six, which ensured greater rigidity between the plates that held the wheel trains in position. The pillars were rivetted to the back plate, but were shaped with shouldered pegs at the other end. These passed through corresponding holes in the front plate where they were pinned in position. A further mark of superior craftsmanship, occasionally found on clocks produced by the better makers, was the use of swivel latches instead of pins to secure the pillars. These fitted into slots in the pillar ends; while they not only facilitated the dismantling of the movement, the latched pillars certainly gave an impression of the clockmaker's pride in his work.

Still further progress was made during the 18th century to improve accuracy in timekeeping. The simple form of Royal pendulum rod, adopted at the time of its invention *c.* 1670, consisted of a length of mild steel wire. In cold weather the rod would contract slightly, thus heightening the pendulum bob a fraction which in turn caused the clock to go a little faster. During a hot summer the reverse would happen and the expansion of the rod would cause the clock to lose time slightly.

To counter this effect, George Graham, a well known and ingenious clockmaker, devised a compensated pendulum which consisted of a jar of mercury in place of the conventional brass-covered pendulum bob. In theory, the expansion of the mercury in hot weather in an upwards direction neutralises the effect of the downwards extension of the pendulum rod, thus maintaining correct time. In cold weather the same result would be achieved, though in reverse. Graham also experimented with a pendulum rod consisting of an arrangement of alternating steel and brass rods. The appearance of this device inspired the name of 'gridiron pendulum'. As the metals had a different coefficient of expansion they could be arranged to cancel one another out in varying temperatures, again maintaining correct timekeeping.

Although Graham apparently did not put the theory of the gridiron compensated pendulum into effect, it was left to a slightly later clockmaker, James Harrison, to do so. James Harrison began life as a joiner and when he turned to clockmaking produced his first movements with wooden wheels, so skilfully made that they worked very well. James was rather overshadowed in reputation by his brother John who has been acclaimed as the most remarkable man in the history of horology, particularly for his work in connection with marine chronometers. Both men worked in Barrow in north Lincolnshire when young; while James remained there, John moved to London when he was forty-two and established himself as a brilliant clockmaker. Research, however, has revealed that James played no small part in the adpatation of the gridiron pendulum, usually credited to his brother. Graham's mercurial bob and Harrison's gridiron pendulum were included in the design of most good regulator clocks well into the late 19th century.

Accurate timekeeping of longcase clocks has become a byword and a proud owner will sometimes regret that more appreciation is not displayed when he exhibits his rather dreadful, badly proportioned and over-decorated clock. Noting a lack of enthusiasm he will invariably say, 'Mind you, it keeps good time.' Of course, a longcase clock in good condition will keep good time, but should there be a tendency for the clock to gain or lose a little it can easily be put right.

Arranging for a longcase clock to keep accurate time is the simplest of operations. Underneath the pendulum bob, which should slide easily on the brass extension to the rod, will be found the rating nut. A turn or two to the right will elevate the bob slightly and the clock will go a little faster. Turn the nut to the left and the bob will descend a fraction and the clock will go slower.

The lack of enthusiasm for thirty-hour clocks in the past has changed in recent times because of the greatly increased prices asked for eight-day clocks. A good thirty-hour clock, which is often smaller and slimmer than its counterpart of longer duration, can often prove a very desirable antique to live with. Unfortunately, some of these clocks have a disturbing feature: when ticking away serenely a somewhat alarming effect may result from the weight suddenly dropping slightly, but with sufficient force to produce an unnerving noise and jarring that will sometimes stop the clock. Again the cure is a simple one. Early thirty-hour longcase clocks were rope-driven while later versions had the weight suspended on a chain. The pulley-wheel over which the rope passed was provided with spikes which caught in the open-woven rope and produced an even movement of the clock mechanism. The later chain-driven clocks also had spiked pulley wheels, but these were provided with thin slots between the spikes into which fitted the alternate links not engaged by the spikes. A clock suffering from this dropping action of the weight was originally rope-driven, but has later had a chain substituted. The chain does not engage properly with a rope-type pulley and a few links will suddenly slip by the spikes thus producing the jolting of the weight. If on examination the pulley-wheel is of the rope type then the chain should be replaced. Specially woven clock ropes may be obtained from clock accessory dealers. Ordinary clothes line or sash window cord is quite unsuitable and should never be used.

Clock weights vary in size according to their purpose and while an eight- or nine-pound weight is sufficient to drive a thirty-hour clock, an eight-day mechanism will require a weight of fourteen or fifteen pounds. Month-going movements require much larger and heavier weights still; one of the factors to be taken into account when deciding the going duration of a longcase clock is the size of the weights. A clock weight much in excess of that required for the purpose should never be used as it is liable to cause very increased wear on the wheel trains and pinions. There is no problem in winding a thirty-hour clock, as the case door has to be opened to gain access to the rope or chain, but it is advisable to support the weight in the free hand while the other is used to pull the rope or chain. When winding an eight-day clock, the case door should always be opened before winding is commenced. This ensures that the weights do not catch in any obstruction and makes certain that they are not wound up too quickly. A weight which is raised carelessly may strike the underside of the seat board and cause a gut-line to break. An eight-day clock may sometimes show a tendency for the gut or wire weight lines to twist together after five or six days' going, which will effectively stop the clock. This means the hole in the seat board, through which the end of the line is knotted, is located too near the barrel that carries the twisted line. It can be corrected by boring a hole further away from the barrel so that the distance between the lines at the top is wider than that lower down when the lines are almost unwound.

The greatest possible care should be taken when moving the clock hands. The minute hand usually moves easily and the hour hand is geared to move with it. If it is necessary to move the hour hand separately, a little extra pressure will normally be sufficient, as the hour hand is designed to be moved in this way. However, if there is the slightest resistance to this it is best to let well alone and have the clock repairer attend to it. Too much force might break it. Similarly, the hand on a one-hand clock is always provided with a counterbalancing tail which should be pressed in one direction with the fingers while the hand itself is being moved in the opposite direction (clockwise).

A third winding hole in a clock dial will indicate a 'ting-tang' or

88. (*Left*) Musical movement of Collier clock showing nest of bells and pinned roller mechanism actuating bell hammers. (*See* pp.85, 86.)

89. (*Above*) Rare false pendulum on longcase organ-clock dial, necessitated by complicated movement prohibiting normal long pendulum. The Lady Lever Art Gallery, Port Sunlight.

quarter-striking movement or possibly a musical clock. Quarter-striking clocks sound two strokes, one on each of two bells, at quarter past the hour, four strokes at the half hour and so on. A musical clock plays a tune at the hour on an octave of small bells which was known in the 18th century as a *'grand sonnerie'*. The Dutch favoured organ clocks where a tune was played on a minia-ture organ fitted to the movement and activated at the hour. The sound is reminiscent of an old-fashioned hurdy-gurdy; although some English clockmakers produced organ clocks they were not as popular as the bell type. In early Victorian times longcase clocks with Cambridge or Whittington chimes were produced. The third winding hole for a chiming or musical clock should always be seen to be symmetrically placed with the other two winding holes. Where it is located in some unusual position (bored through the chapter ring, for instance), this will indicate that the musical part of the movement has been added at a later date.

CHAPTER ELEVEN

Elementary Repairs and Maintenance

THERE SHOULD BE no misunderstanding the very real importance of placing a longcase clock needing repair in the hands of a competent and professional restorer. Nowadays, more and more well trained craftsmen are setting up in business, but only a few years ago fine clocks were too often entrusted to the inadequate skills of some amateur 'clock doctor'. A botched-up job usually resulted, sometimes with irreparable damage being done. I recall one old watch and clock repairer who had a sovereign remedy for all the ailments of antique longcase-clock movements. He simply removed the hands and dial and immersed the movement in a bucket of paraffin oil. He next hung it up to dry out for a few hours and then put a touch of clock oil at the end of the arbors or spindles. In most instances, the clock would go again for another delighted customer and the great thing was that no harm had been done. The old man would never do anything more, as he once confided in me that there was no money in antique-clock repairing, even if he could have done it, because it took too long.

One of the more common defects in a longcase clock occurs when the lunar movement or the calendar is not working. Closer inspection behind the dial will reveal that the toothed wheels actuating the trip mechanisms for these devices have been removed. This was another easy 'cure' favoured by the unscrupulous repairer. Continuous going over many years will wear the leaves of the pinions, enlarge the arbor holes and wear the pallets on the anchor escapement. The movement would eventually 'give up the ghost' and refuse to go; removing one or both of the actuating wheels for the moon and calendar mechanisms would slightly lessen the load on the going train to a degree which permitted the clock to go again for a few more years.

There are, however, a few simple 'first aid' operations which the amateur collector may carry out and which may help to start a clock going again. Because a clock movement is a machine some of the moving parts must be oiled from time to time. Long neglect will have caused the lubrication to dry out, which will cause the clock to stop. A light brush over with a volatile solvent like petrol or lighter fuel will remove the old, dried oil, which forms a sort of gum. Fresh oil can then be applied, but it is important that it be applied only to the ends of the arbors or spindles where they turn in the small holes in the front and back plates of the movement. A touch of oil on the surfaces of the anchor pallets and a little where the brass square at the top of the pendulum rod slides in the fork of the crutch will also help the clock go more smoothly. Do not oil the toothed wheels or the pinions; this will cause dust to adhere, in time forming a sticky mess which will clog the wheel trains. A good clock oil should be used for preference, but a refined domestic machine oil will suffice (applied in small droplets from the end of a piece of wire). Olive oil should on no account be applied as this is a vegetable oil which will soon coagulate and further 'gum up the works'.

Serious damage may be caused to a longcase clock by careless or ignorant handling during a house removal or when it is required to move a longcase clock to another situation in the house. It would be foolhardy to attempt to move the clock with all its various parts in position. A simple drill or routine carried out in an orderly sequence is all that is necessary. First, the hood is removed; the clock should be wound almost fully and then the weights unhooked. Winding before the weights are taken away will ensure that the gut or wire lines do not tangle. Next the pendulum is lifted from the slot in the pendulum cock and finally the seat board, to which the movement and dial is attached, is lifted clear from the case.

If the clock is to be moved a considerable distance then all the parts should be carefully wrapped and placed in cardboard boxes. Early brass-covered weights are very vulnerable, as the old brass covering is likely to peel off if subjected to any shock or rough handling. The pendulum should be tied to a length of wood to protect the fine spring 'feather' at the top of the pendulum rod; this too can easily be bent or broken.

To set the clock up again in its new location the dismantling process must be carried out in reverse. Do not hang the weights without first checking that the lines have not become entangled in the wheel trains. When finally assembled and going smoothly the longcase should be screwed to the wall. If not secured longcase clocks can topple over and a dreadful tragedy ensue; an examination of the back board of the clock will usually reveal a number of old screw holes where this fixing operation has been carried out after many moves over the years.

Sometimes a longcase clock may be seen leaning perilously to one side like the Tower of Pisa because a piece of wood or a block has been placed under one corner of the base to tilt it. The owner will explain that the clock will only go when this is done. This is quite a dangerous situation to permit and may cause the clock to fall over, quite apart from the incongruous spectacle the clock presents. All that should be done is to return the clock to a vertical position and to 'set it in beat'; this will produce that soothing, even, ticking sound which is such a pleasant characteristic of an old longcase clock.

To carry out this operation, the clock should be perfectly upright and not going. Having opened the case door, a pencil mark should be made on the back board at a point where the end of the pendulum hangs motionless. The pendulum is then moved to one side, very gently and slowly until the 'tick' sound is heard and another pencil mark is placed on the back board at the point of the pendulum's end. Now, with great care, the pendulum is moved over to the other side until the 'tock' is audible; a further pencil mark is recorded. If the clock is 'in beat' the distances from the 'tick' and 'tock' marks to the centre mark should be equal. If not, then the clock will tick unevenly and will probably not go at all. The remedy is to bend the pendulum crutch, which is made specially of soft iron for this purpose, very slightly in the direction of the shorter pencil-marked space. This may prove something of a trial-and-error operation, but an even ticking sound can soon be achieved by a very slight bending of the crutch wire.

Due to careless handling, the pendulum 'feather' or thin suspension spring is sometimes broken. Replacement feathers are easily obtainable from clock and watch spare parts dealers who are listed in the *Yellow Pages*. Sometimes, 'feathers' are supplied with small rectangular brass blocks with tapped holes so that they can be screwed onto the top end of the pendulum rod. Alternatively, the broken 'feather' can be removed from the old block by punching out the pin that holds it, using a hammer and centre punch or sharp nail. A slight variation in the length of the new 'feather' may require an adjustment of the fast/slow rating nut at the end of the pendulum rod.

Another straight-forward repair job is the replacement of broken weight lines on an eight-day clock. Although only one line may have snapped it is better to replace the two as the other may break soon after. Coils of gut are sold by clock accessory suppliers to provide an amount sufficient for two new lines.

Nowadays, nylon lines are sometimes substituted for gut; phosphor bronze or steel wire lines have been in use for many years. The latter, however, entail some soldering when being connected up and are not so manageable as the traditional gut lines in the hands of an amateur. Having dismantled the clock, as already

90. Movement of Windmills' clock showing latched plates and gut line secured by knot in side hole of 'going' barrel.

described for a removal, one broken end of the gut line is removed from the seat board where it has been knotted through a hole. The other end has to be removed from a small hole in the barrel drum and here a pair of tweezers is helpful. The gut can be pushed out through another hole in the side of the barrel where it will be found to have a knot in the end. Thread the new gut through the hole in the drum of the barrel so that it comes out through the side hole. Now tie a single small knot in the gut end and burn off any excess gut beyond the knot with a match. The knotted end is then pulled into the barrel through the side hole where it will be secure and not impede the movement in any way. Remember to thread the gut through the wire loop on the weight pulley wheel and then knot the free end through the hole in the seat board. Sometimes the knot is tied round a short steel pin or nail to prevent it being pulled through the hole by the force of the weight.

All chapter rings were originally silvered as were the calendar rings on brass dial clocks. Where the silvering has been rubbed away by too enthusiastic dusting, it can be restored by a simple chemical operation which was the original method in use as early as the end of the 17th century. Silvered parts on an antique clock should never be electro-plated. Having removed the chapter ring from the dial by extracting the pins from the brass holding pegs, clean it with a small cotton wool pad soaked in household ammonia; this will remove patches of old discoloured lacquer. The ammonia should be applied out of doors. Complete the cleaning with a light rubbing action using a small block of toilet pumice. This should be done with a sweeping movement following with the curve of the chapter ring and so provide a fine continuous grain in the brass.

Dissolve a few small crystals of silver nitrate, obtainable from any large chemist store, in a small glass or test tube of water. Silver nitrate is corrosive and very poisonous and should be handled with care. Next dissolve a similar quantity of common salt in water and add it to the silver nitrate solution. Immediately a precipitate of silver chloride will occur and this will settle to the bottom of the vessel. The liquid should be poured away and the silver chloride washed several times.

The substance is now ready for re-silvering the chapter ring. First rub a little damp common salt over the surface and then wash off. Next take small, equal parts of silver chloride and ordinary cream of tartar and mix with a very small amount of water, just sufficient to make a paste. Take some of the paste on a small damp cotton wool pad and rub gently over the surface of the chapter ring. Immediately a greyish, blue deposit of silver will appear on the brass and this operation should be continued until all the area has been treated. Now wash the ring under a tap and with another clean pad of cotton wool rub it gently with moist cream of tarter only.

The silver deposit will lose its dark blue colour and will present a bright, silvery appearance. The deposit is extremely thin and will not stand up to polishing so having dried off any moisture remaining on the chapter ring, warm it slightly and give the newly silvered surface a thin coat of colourless, metal lacquer. This should be applied with a soft camel-hair brush, which will protect the silvered surface for many years.

The delicate, hand-sawn fretwork on early, mild steel clock hands makes them very susceptible to breakage. If this does occur the hands should be silver-soldered and this is a job for an expert. Soft or lead soldering is not satisfactory. Old steel hands were never painted and where this has been done the paint has probably been used to conceal a repair. In order to present a darker appearance against the brass dial and silvered chapter ring, hands were given a dark-blue colour by heating gently on a small tray of sand. Again, the clock accessory dealer will help, as a 'blueing' solution can be bought in a small bottle and applied to the hand to give the required colour. Here it must be said that those who are timorous of attempting the silvering process described above may also obtain a silvering solution ready prepared and which produces quite a satisfactory result.

It has already been said that many people are not happy with a rope- or chain-drive thirty-hour clock. Daily winding becomes a chore and easily overlooked and consequently the poor old clock is left in a run-down state. If the owner of this type of longcase clock is prepared to eliminate the hourly striking then the clock can be made to go for up to four days and thus only be required to be wound twice a week. This can be done by removing the lifting piece, a small steel arm which actuates the striking mechanism. It is a simple procedure of taking out the little pin which holds the

91. Thirty-hour clock movement with lifting piece (above wheels), the removal of which will prolong going time.

lifting piece on the squared end of an arbor, situated usually on the top right hand of the front plate of the movement. The lifting piece can be put back at any time and the striking of the hours will re-commence but, of course, the clock will only go for thirty hours again. It is wise to attach the lifting piece to the seat board with wire so that it doesn't get mislaid.

The majority of repairs to the casework, such as replacing parts missing from the hood pediment or adding a new plinth to restore a clock to its correct height after having been cut down at some time, are tasks for an expert woodworker. Nevertheless, simple restoration of missing patches of veneer where these are not too large, or cross-banding, is not a difficult matter for the amateur.

Small sheets of veneer of the correct type of wood can be obtained from hobby or craft shops; but, in this modern age the veneer will be machine-cut and very thin. Antique veneers were sawn by hand and therefore thicker; the discrepancy in thickness can be overcome by using two or three thicknesses of the new veneer, glued together. The area of veneer to be restored should be carefully cleaned of old glue and trimmed to a definite shape with a sharp craft knife. The veneer to be fitted is then cut to size and tried in position to ascertain that it fits well. Having glued the veneer in position it should be held in place until the adhesive is dry by strapping down with cellotape, which can later be removed. A gentle rub down with fine glasspaper and a thin coat of brown French polish or 'knotting' will restore the colour; when the brushed-on polish is dry it can be waxed.

Much interesting detail on the longcase itself, such as fine stringing or inlay, is sometimes hidden by a covering of old varnish. As this is usually very dry and brittle it can be removed by rubbing with fine wire wool. Always rub in the direction of the grain of the wood as any motion across the grain may cause scratching. Finish off by treating as for newly applied veneer or cross-banding.

Such repairs to the movement as re-bushing arbor holes, the replacement of missing teeth from the wheel trains or fitting new pallets to a worn anchor escapement are all jobs for the professional restorer and should not be attempted by an amateur, unless he or she has had some training and possesses a well-equipped workshop. Longcase clocks are rare and, for the most part, beautiful examples of applied and decorative art and should be treated with great respect.

CHAPTER TWELVE

Fakes, Forgeries and Reproductions

As with most forms of fine and decorative art, it has become worthwhile for the faker and the forger to exercise their skills in the field of antique longcase clocks. It is not always realised that there is a very real difference in the activities of these nefarious characters. The forger sets out to make a complete copy of a clock by some famous maker whose work is in great demand and accordingly fetches very high prices. His task is often a very difficult one because he has to reproduce the known characteristics in the work of a particular maker with all the signs of having been made centuries ago, yet this must not be overdone. The distressing of wooden casework and metal ornaments presents few problems. It is the spurious wear on pinions and wheels, the unnecessary re-bushing of arbor holes and all those small indications of age which take up the forger's time and skill.

The faker is in a rather different category as he is after easier, if not so substantial, rewards for his dubious skills. Briefly, his job is to 'improve' a simple, but originally genuine, antique clock, usually the work of some ordinary provincial maker, and to turn it into something which will catch the eye of the collector.

Some years ago I made the acquaintance of two dealers who were in partnership together. They were a likeable pair, but not above suspicion. One day I found a longcase clock in their shop which had a very large case and a painted arch dial. In the arch was a painting of a paddle steamer which was also equipped with sails. This indicated a fairly late date of manufacture in the 19th century. One dealer remarked that it was a pity that the ship was a paddle steamer as a sailing clipper would have made a quick sale more likely. A few days later the clock was gone and the dealers could not suppress their glee in confessing that they had painted out the funnels on the ship. A short time after the same clock was back in the shop again; the unsuccessful fakers ruefully admitted that while they had carefully obliterated the funnels they had omitted to remove the paddle wheels.

This incident might seem a trivial effort at deception but a far more serious example of faking is concerned with the removal of a minor clockmaker's name from an engraved brass dial and the substitution of a more famous one. Formerly this was done by carefully 'stoning out' the original name and although the engraved letters might have appeared to have been quite deeply cut, patient rubbing with an abrasive stone could eradicate them. The only sure way of detecting this operation, if suspicion is aroused, is to hold the dial in a horizontal position and look along the surface when the very shallow depression caused by the stoning can be observed. I have seen a dial so treated with the newly engraved inscription of 'Thomas Tompion Londini fecit'. To anyone who appreciated the distinguishing features of a fine, early longcase clock it would have been obvious that this specimen belonged to a period long after the great London clockmaker had departed from this world. Furthermore, such a clock would never have been produced in his workshop.

A very minor deceit, in a way excusable, is where a dial and movement have been transferred to a case which was not the original one. This is known as a 'married clock'. Walnut veneer and oak and a number of other woods are often found to have been seriously damaged by woodworm which may have been done a long time ago. The ravages of the powder beetle have caused some clock cases to disintegrate completely. The old clockmakers, unless they ran very large establishments, did not make their own clock cases, but ordered them from a casemaker. In fact, some smaller details like the shape of the hinges and the similarity of marquetry patterns indicate that some early clockmakers must have employed the same casemakers for years.

Small longcase clocks with brass dials have always been very much sought after; to satisfy the demand the obliging faker has resorted to a fairly common piece of trickery. One-handed clocks have never been very popular, except with dedicated antiquarian horologists, because a great number of people say that they cannot tell the time by them. Clocks which must be wound every day have never been so attractive to the majority of people as those which will go for a week or eight days. During the greater part of the 18th

92. (*Left*) Original 18th-century one-hand thirty-hour longcase clock converted to two-hand eight-day clock. 93. (*Right, top*) Dial of converted clock without minute band and numerals indicating original use with one hand only. 94. (*Right, bottom*) Dial of faked marquetry clock (*see* p.123) showing period characteristics nearly 100 years later than those of case: no quarter hour markings on inside edge of chapter ring; arc of circle date opening; spandrels are typical of second half 18th-century pattern; early 19th-century type hour and minute hands.

century a considerable number of country-made longcase clocks were produced with small, square brass dials and short, narrow cases, mostly in oak. To the disappointment of the uninformed clock hunter these small clocks nearly always have one hand and a going duration of thirty hours. What could be easier for the faker than to take an eight-day, two-handed movement, usually from a white-dial clock, and attach it to the small, square brass dial in the attractively slim case. Holes can be bored in the dial for the winding squares without difficulty; to the knowledgeable collector these all too common fakes are obvious: the one-handed clock has quarter hour marks only engraved on the inner edge of the chapter ring; there are no minute marks for the newly applied minute hand after the faker's work is done. It is surprising how many people live with these attractive little frauds for years and never suspect the deception that has been perpetrated.

Another, not quite so obvious fake, is where an eight-day movement has been transferred to a thirty-hour, two-handed dial. Winding holes can be bored in the exact position required and the only tell-tale evidence of the switch is where an inspection behind the dial will reveal that the pillars for joining the dial to the movement have been sawn off and soldered into new positions to match the holes in the front plate of the replacement movement.

Some fakes, however, were carried out in Georgian times. So long as the dial and movement can be put into a genuine case of the same period with an exact fit, then the change-over can scarcely be faulted or even be seen to have been done. It is when a 'marriage' is arranged with an early clock being placed in a much later case that the new alliance becomes questionable. Thus an early 18th-century clock in a case with a swan-neck pediment on the hood would be completely wrong. Late-Georgian square brass dials have occasionally been seen in cases where the hood has been designed to take an arch-dial clock, the empty space above the square dial being filled with a wooden panel. A reversal of this obvious counterfeit occurs when the arch and lunar movement have been cut away, reducing the dial to a square shape so that it would fit into an empty available case originally intended for a square-dial clock.

Casemakers always made a frame or dial surround, sometimes referred to as a bezel, inside the hood which fitted the dial exactly.

95. Longcase by Hampson
of Warrington.
Characteristics of dial and
case suggest this is a
'married' clock.

Where a clock with a smaller dial has been introduced, then a smaller inner bezel is sometimes added to fill the space around the dial. This should arouse suspicion immediately. Alternatively, the dial surround may have been removed altogether and this should indicate that a 'marriage' has taken place.

Fakers sometimes forget little points, like a hood door that has no trace of an iron locking staple ever having been fitted to the inside of the lower rail, but a slot to take a staple is present in the wooden dial surround. A further check might reveal the presence of a bolt inside the case near the top to lock the staple and so prevent the hood door being opened; however no slot appears in the dial surround. In this instance a very careful check of the hood door is called for, as it is probably a replacement and the faker has over-looked the detail of the locking device.

A simple form of deception was practised by some north-country clockmakers in the 18th century when they produced thirty-hour longcase clocks with dummy winding squares and holes in the dial, thus giving the appearance of an eight-day clock. Thirty-hour clocks were cheaper than the eight-day variety, but the possession of one of the latter type was probably a minor Georgian status symbol. This little domestic sham is comparable with the bogus hallmarks used on early Victorian plated tableware. These longcase clocks with dummy winding holes used to be quite common; however, occasionally an example is met where a faker has exchanged the thirty-hour movement for an eight-day one. It was very unlikely that the winding squares on the new movement would fit exactly the winding holes on the thirty-hour dial so these would be enlarged, almost imperceptibly, to one side of the hole or the other. Nevertheless, an experienced collector would spot the attempted fake.

The faking of casework is more unusual, but some considerable expertise was used in the early part of the present century in veneering and adding bird-and-flower marquetry to an otherwise plain case. An examination of one longcase marquetry clock re-vealed that, while the interior of the case had all the marks of antiquity and was genuinely old, the longcase door was quite new, the whole piece being covered in fine walnut veneer and the door with panels of bird-and-flower marquetry. But here again, the faker had made a 'give-away' mistake. All doors of longcase clocks are made from solid wood with the grain running length-wise. In order to prevent warping, battens about two inches in width, are fitted across each end of the door with tongue-and-groove joints. These form a perfectly flat surface onto which the marquetry or veneer can be glued. In a genuine old door, the battens nearly always shrink over the years, causing the veneer to tear in a thin ragged line at the top and bottom of the door. The faker would find it very difficult to imitate this crack even if he had remembered to do so. The moral in this particular instance is to be very suspicious of veneered longcase clocks that have no hori-zontal cracks in the door.

Other attempts to fake an antique appearance include inserting

96. (*Left*) Original longcase covered with fake (modern) bird-and-flower marquetry. A new case door has been added. 97. (*Right*) One-hand thirty-hour clock by Berry, Hitchen, *c.* 1725; lenticle does not coincide with pendulum bob.

98. Horizontal tear in marquetry due to batten shrinkage in construction at lower end of longcase door.

side windows in the hood or lenticles in the door where none have existed before. These are not easy to detect, because genuine lenticles do appear in country-made oak cases where the little window does not coincide with the pendulum bob, suggesting that the casemaker did not really understand the purpose of the lenticle. The cross-banded beading of a flat oval section placed around the long case doors of late 17th- and early 18th-century clocks, veneered in walnut and marquetry, is sometimes found to be partly missing. Ruthless restorers will occasionally remove all the remaining beading and substitute lengths of straight conventional moulding of stepped-curve section or similar shape in its place. This observation may appear over-critical of the restorer's efforts but, nevertheless, an early longcase clock, particularly one in a walnut case, is worthy of the most meticulous replacement of every missing part exactly as it should be.

Clock hands are delicate things and easily broken; one of the saddest spectacles is to see a fine early 18th-century dial with a pair of black-enamelled, stamped-brass hands, later in period by one hundred years, replacing the originals. Far better to seek the services of an expert clock restorer to obtain a hand-cut pair of the correct period which will match exactly the design of the dial. Worst of all is to see plain, black spear-shaped hands on a brass dial. They really do stand out like 'sore thumbs'.

Probably one of the most dreadful acts of vandalism ever to be perpetrated on a longcase clock was covering the entire case with carving in high and low relief at a later date. This was often done in Victorian times when anything old had to be made to look even older and more romantic by covering every available space with pseudo-antique carving. It did, in fact, become a pastime for the ladies of leisure who, with their little chip-carving knives and sets of carving tools, did irreparable damage to many fine early 18th-century pieces of antique furniture.

There is a human and commendable loyalty often displayed by the owner of a longcase clock. Generally, it is held that all grandfather clocks must be very, very old and it only requires the conversation to veer round to the subject of clocks for the most

99. Detail of carved decoration on converted clock added during so-called 'Romantic' period.

astounding attributes to be claimed on behalf of the family long-case. Following an article I once wrote for the press about an interesting brass dial clock which I had come across, the editor was assailed by letters from all around proclaiming the great age of respective clocks. Naturally, the editor was delighted and the correspondence column was spattered with clocks letters for weeks. One lady, loud in the praise of her clock, maintained that it was Elizabethan because it had a carved profile of Elizabeth I on the case door and, moreover, it had a white dial. Profound ignorance on both scores had been manifested. On the first count there were, of course, no longcase clocks in the days of Good Queen Bess. They had not yet been invented and white or painted dials did not appear until *c*. 1760 when the good queen had been dead some 157 years. The carved head had probably been added by somebody in a fit of Victorian Romanticism.

This is not to say that all carved longcases are the work of later fakers, however innocent, because a few casemakers in mid-Georgian times did elaborate their designs with some usually restrained carving which was always in the style of the period in which the cases were produced. Nevertheless, a carved longcase should always be examined thoroughly to ascertain whether it is genuine or not. I recollect a longcase clock belonging to a friend of mine which had an attractive brass arch dial with a lunar movement. The hands, unfortunately, were obviously not of the correct period and the dark oak case was decorated all over with low relief lunettes and other fan-shaped carvings. One day I had the opportunity of examining the case door more closely and found that the carving and subsequent staining had almost concealed the fact that originally the case doors and base panel had been cross-banded with mahogany into which the carver's chisel had cut in a number of places. This indicated, without doubt, that the carved decoration was a considerably later addition.

The great rarity of a genuine grandmother clock has provoked one particularly ingenious form of fake. In this instance, the faker had taken a wall longcase clock, like the type mentioned in Chapter Seven, adding a conventional base so that the clock would stand on the floor. In fact, the only faked part was the base, which few people would have examined anyway, the rest of the clock being perfectly genuine in every detail.

Electric longcase clocks, designed as such, are interesting and often very collectable items; however, an original weight-driven clock which has had the movement and weights removed and an electrical system put in its place is a very sad thing to behold. In fact, it would reflect seriously on the good taste of the owner who would give house room to such a monstrosity. It is doubtful whether a faker of even mediocre talent would stoop so low as to 'electrocute a grandfather'.

Whenever a shortage of genuine antique longcase clocks occurs, some dealers are prepared to offer modern reproductions on sale. Some of these are very attractive clocks with movements made in Germany and Scandinavia, the wooden cases being produced in Italy. Designs are usually traditional and although the movements bear little resemblance to those of the old longcase clocks, many of them are weight-driven and have long pendulums. The design of the dials, including spandrels and hands, is based on earlier patterns and the shape of many of the hood tops follows that of the swan-neck pediment in many cases. Smaller than the average antique longcase clock, they are larger than the so-called reproduction 'grandmother' type; although not cheap, are not nearly so expensive as the real thing. For those who cannot afford an antique longcase clock then these reproductions, many of which have chiming movements, make very attractive and companionable alternatives. It is as well to recall that all antique longcase clocks were once new and fresh from the clockmaker's shop, smelling of newly oiled metal parts and the tang of woodwork just from the bench.

'How can fakes and forgeries be avoided?' the would-be collector of longcase clocks may enquire. The answer is to purchase from a well-known, accredited dealer in antique clocks. You may have to pay a little more, but that is for his expertise in providing you with the genuine article.

If you are going to risk the hazards of the sale room and the junk shop, then you must do your homework first. Learn all you can from authoritative, specialist books on the subject and by visiting collections in museums and art galleries. It may take longer this way, but every minute will be enjoyable and well spent.

Index

N.B.: Page numbers in *italic* refer to illustrations where these are separated from the text.

ACKNOWLEDGEMENTS

The author and publishers wish to express their appreciation to a number of individuals for making available clocks from their collections to be photographed for this book, and to Colin Pitcher for taking many of the photographs. They are grateful to the Trustees of the Lady Lever Art Gallery, Port Sunlight and to the University of Liverpool for their kindly cooperation.

Illustrations

NB Numbers refer to illustration numbers. The photographs were taken for the Hamlyn Group by Colin Pitcher, with the exception of the following:

Author 50, 82, 83; British Museum, London 17, 28, 58, 64; Christies, London 13, 14; Photographie Giraudon, Paris 67; Greenfield Village and the Henry Ford Museum, Dearborn, Michigan 70; Hamlyn Group Picture Library 10, 53, 60, 65; Wallace Collection, London 68; Worshipful Company of Clockmakers, London 27; Wuppertal Clock Museum 72, 73; Yale University Art Gallery 71.

Illustration 16 is reproduced by Gracious Permission of Her Majesty the Queen.

Publisher's Note: The drawings on p.98 are by the author.